BREAK THROUGH *the* NOISE

9 TOOLS to *PROPEL* YOUR MARKETING MESSAGE

ELISA SOUTHARD

Walnut Creek, CA

Published by MarketSkills Publications
1233 Alpine Road, Suite 203
Walnut Creek, CA 94596

Publisher's Cataloguing-in-Publication Data
Southard, Elisa
　　Break through the noise : 9 tools to propel your marketing message / Elisa
　　Southard. –Walnut Creek, CA : MarketSkills Publications, 2004.

　　　p. ; cm.

　　ISBN: 0-9744892-0-4
　　1. Marketing. 2. Relationship marketing. I. Title.

HF5415 .S68 2004　　　2003114440
658.8–dc22　　　　　　0311

Book coordination by Jenkins Group, Inc. • www.bookpublishing.com
Interior design by Barbara Hodge
Cover design by Chris Rhoads
Editor, Deborah Grossman
Interior illustrations by Trina Swerdlow, B.F.A.
Associate art director, Mary Lou Thiercof
Author photographer, Michael Mejia

Printed in the United States of America

07 06 05 04 03 • 5 4 3 2 1

Dedicated to...

You, the reader, whose time and talent propel interest. As you turn these pages, may your interest turn into abundant opportunities.

Acknowledgments

In the spirit of Bob Dylan's song, "If Not for You..." thank you:

Will Southard, early reader, forever partner, who carries dreams in his pockets the way most people carry change. Through your actions you remind me daily life is art, and you helped me integrate a deeper sense of aesthetics onto these pages. Thanks for urging me to have fun with it.

Arte Maren, upon whose ears the *Break Through the Noise* concept first fell over pastrami sandwiches at Max's Opera Cafe. Your contributions to early ideas, concepts and co-piloting the initial outline made it possible.

Joe Barnett, I see you in your studio, mixing the *Break Through the Noise* theme song as only you can do. Thank you for your continuing creativity in helping me bond information with entertainment.

Gretchen Givens, thank you for synthesizing the thoughts and ideas of our conversations over the years into the *Break Through the Noise* theme song. With its easy-to-sing words and wonderful percussion, you captured the full spirit of the manuscript.

Deborah Grossman, your impeccable editing, organizing and summarizing gave these concepts a life of their own. Whether we worked in the office conference room or sipped our favorite beverages throughout the Bay Area, the ideas always flowed. Thank you.

Rob Healy, thank you for sharing your personal *Break Through the Noise* story to make these concepts accessible and alive.

Jay Hoyer and Marcie Hochhauser of the Walnut Creek Chamber of Commerce, chamber executives extraordinaire. Thank you for your ever-present enthusiasm and for your ideas and referrals, especially during the research phase.

Laurie Jessup, I'm still speechless over the jeweled hammers you sent so casually in the mail. Thank you for making the tool theme sparkle.

Penny Melrose, your laughter and perspective helped me see

beyond the pages. Thank you for assisting with the promotional materials.

Rich Moore and Dave Baker, the seed for this book was planted when we worked together, and many opportunities I have today trace back to our association. As sentimental as it sounds, you put me in the path of success. Thank you.

Trina Swerdlow, illustrator, who took concepts from the text and turned them into personalities.

Mary Lou Thiercof, guardian angel of design. Thank you for taking me to Home Depot for materials to make a custom toolkit, for designing the original booklets, and associate art-directing images throughout the book.

Peggy White of the Diablo Regional Arts Association, thank you for all the opportunities to bring my marketing skills into play and bridge my twin loves of business and the arts.

Lindsey Wolf of the Public Relations Society of America, thank you for helping me achieve a career milestone, an accreditation in public relations, APR. The APR discipline was invaluable for the research of this book.

Thank you readers and test marketers for your feedback, Catherine Bergeron, Mike Cavanagh, Linda Childers, Drew Johnston, Barbara Koeth, Vernie Laube, Terry Mahaley, Marge Michaels, Pete Michaels, Sue Polgar, Kaer Southard and Vanessa Valentine.

Thank you to all the professionals on these pages, for sharing your insights, experience and expertise.

To Drew, Haley Rose, Maeve, and Maighread, thank you for your uplifting smiles throughout the process.

Thank you, Len, dear brother, for sharing resources and setting an example to pursue my passions with style and humor.

And thank you to Rich, Glenn, Susie, Steve, Bill and everyone in my office building. You participated in every survey along the way, and I'll miss the kidding about watching *Oprah* when I was at home writing.

Contents

If you view marketing as difficult, distracting, and time consuming, this chapter provides ways to plug into a marketing frame of mind without disrupting your routine.

You've reached the stage where production and income plateau. Unless you take risks to expand, your business will contract.

This chapter addresses what happens if you become content with "keeping things the same." We explore how to put something at stake and take action to ensure its success.

It's time to achieve consistent results with daily actions. This chapter reveals how to identify and sustain successful activities to keep your marketing going.

Chapter Four: *Get a Grip*

It's noisy out in the community. Now is the time to get an immediate grip on your prospective client's attention and interest. This chapter explores what it takes to break through the noise of competition and short attention spans with a tool called the "Talking Tagline."

Chapter Five: *Gauge Receptivity*

How well do you assess prospective client receptivity under the stress of a marketing situation? In this chapter you will boost your ability to read signals and gauge needs through conversation, observation and inquiry.

Chapter Six: *Nail It Down*

Building and managing messages is key to communicating the essence of your values and services. Here you learn how to craft messages and create credibility, flexibility and heritage.

Chapter Seven: *Stretch Out*

How do you keep significant people in your space without sacrificing one more thing—without adding one more expense? This chapter demonstrates how to extend a concept, and never run out of original ideas to stretch dialogue over time.

Chapter Eight: *Get Sticky*

What's the best way to multiply awareness for your services without incurring substantial marketing costs? This chapter explains how to turn stories into professional recommendations.

Chapter Nine: *Recharge*

What are the signs its time to recharge your marketing approach? This chapter examines the entire step-by-step Break Through the Noise™ process. You can assess which skills to recharge.

Fanmail for You?

As you read *Break Through the Noise,* your attitude will attract marketing opportunities. Your messages will be more alive and active, thereby inviting action, and you'll know you can count on your approach under pressure.

I'm one of your biggest fans, so please share your stories using these tools. Send an e-mail to *success@marketskills.com.* I'd love to hear all about it.

Let's Get Acquainted

"I'm in," Rich Moore said as he looked over at Dave Baker, who was probably thinking about baseball. The happiest years of Dave's young adulthood were spent crouched behind home plate—catcher's mitt on alert. He was no stranger to deciding his next move quickly. He had already made up his mind.

"Me, too."

It was the end of the year, and the two accounting professionals, friends in their youth, partners in their prime, smiled as their plane touched down at San Francisco International Airport. They had just returned from an industry retreat. Now, their New Year's resolution was in place. They would add to their accounting firm something that is commonplace today. At that time, this element was as green as the proverbial eyeshade.

What they reached for was an adventure, regardless of the stage of any business. They were ahead of the curve for the inevitable—formalizing marketing and public relations efforts.

That's where I came in. Rich and Dave were the accountants for several of my clients. I was ready for a change. And New Year's seemed the perfect time to make one.

The next three years were busy. We restructured proposals; trained in-house staff; launched a newsletter; chaired committees; hosted community meetings; authored articles; and launched, with Dave as chair, one of the most successful, if not the county's first, golf fundraisers to benefit multiple charities. Outreach activities, materials, and participation in the community swelled.

Almost three years to the month after their giving high fives with "I'm in," the firm received the prestigious Pacific Bell Small Business Achievement Award. Looking back, this event culminated our work and led to the start of my professional marketing/public relations practice—with Moore & Baker as my first client.

What I learned from helping these top professionals discover their hidden marketing talents is this: Marketing, the nine-letter word that describes all those messages, materials, and activities that promote your business and stimulate demand for it, should be easy! And fun! And simple!

Thus, my mission, my raison d'etre, if you will, is to make marketing accessible, simple, and enjoyable for technically-oriented professionals.

Since the days I sat at the conference table with Rich and Dave and their team, I've shared marketing messages and techniques with thousands of professionals, from those in private practice and non-profit settings to those in academia and the arts.

For over a decade, I've coached professionals one-to-one, spoken at annual conferences, moderated in-house training sessions, and participated in roundtables to entice business owners to dust off marketing projects abandoned in their credenza drawer.

I've schlepped flip charts in the early-morning hours to spread the word to executives, accompanied clients to their initial outreach event, and connected business owners with broad-based contacts. I've witnessed their marketing dreams come alive, as they enhance their communities, and propel their businesses into new levels of income.

One timeless trait towers above the rest.

As a technical professional, whether you help clients lower taxes, build wealth, alleviate pain, fix smiles, or find a new home or career, you'd often prefer to engage in activities other than promoting yourself. And when you do, you want marketing to be simple, easy, and enjoyable.

I feel the same. With the tools you'll pick up on these pages, you'll market with the same ease you slip into the garage early on Saturday morning, pick up your favorite gear—be it a golf club, a sander, or even a guitar pick—and power up without thinking twice.

I wrote this book to answer the deeper question: Along with ease, how could you market your services in a style that doesn't compromise your professional stature or consume a significant budget or consume your most precious commodity—time?

Break Through the Noise
An Alternative to Traditional Marketing

Over the past decade, bandwidth became cheaper and wider. Companies poured millions of dollars into sophisticated electronic marketing and advertising programs and delivered millions of messages to you and your clients every second of every minute across multiple media—hundreds of cable channels, handheld devices, radio, television, pop-up windows, pop-behind windows, and, with a nod to pedestrian shoppers, storefront windows.

Innately, you knew throwing more dollars at advertising only added to the crushing noise.

In the time we will spend together, we'll look at alternatives to traditional marketing. You'll gain new skills and brush up on some you've encountered before. Through stories, case studies, and practical activities, this book stands on the same foundation you used to build your technical skills—a logical yet flexible approach—and converts your technical skills into marketing skills step by step.

How to Use This Book

Here's a quick reference to the skills you'll gain as you *break through the noise.*

Power Up: Plug In, Raise the Stakes, Tee Off

These tools get you into a marketing frame of mind. They ensure you have a game to play with enough challenge to stimulate and sustain your interest.

Build Messages: Get a Grip, Gauge Receptivity, Nail It Down

These tools take you out into the community. With them, you build messages that communicate your worth and relationships that nurture what you value.

Recharge Energy: Stretch Out, Get Sticky, Recharge

As your practice grows, it's tempting to slack off and let successful activities slide. These tools nudge you to take nothing for granted and use your time to your greatest advantage.

Whether you are a marketing veteran or a professional starting a new practice or new service, you're in control of your pace and progress.

Here are a few suggestions.

Are you:	Check out:
Launching a new practice or transitioning from a corporate career	"Plug In"
Stalled or haven't marketed in a while	"Raise the Stakes"
Struggling to get started	"Tee Off"
Bored going to business functions	"Get a Grip"
Hesitating to introduce your services	"Gauge Receptivity"
Tongued-tied or too wordy	"Nail It Down"
Drained of new ideas	"Stretch Out"
Out of touch with contacts	"Get Sticky"
Not sure where to start	"Recharge"

As you turn the pages, read the stories, and put pen to paper for these MarketSkills, you'll find it easier and easier to get out from behind your desk and become a player in the marketing game you knew was inevitable.

We're at the end of the beginning. It's time to *Break Through the Noise*. It's time to turn the page.

Let's get busy,
Elisa Southard

CHAPTER ONE

Plug In

What's his secret? Bill Collins shared his story with me. In retirement, he traveled around the world every morning by 10 a.m. He often said, "It's amazing what's out there. It gives me a new perspective on how we live, how others think."

After 25 years of sipping his morning coffee in a radio booth while spinning top country songs, he stirred his coffee with a splash of webcam.com.

Camera eyes took him across continents and then onto street corners and into phone booths and building entrances—like an opening movie scene.

It reminds me of the movie classic *Casablanca*, which opens with a slow-spinning globe. The camera moves slowly to Paris on a world map where against a backdrop of World War II refugees traveling by auto, train, and foot, a dark, thick line flows their route across land and sea onto the African continent and into Casablanca. The camera then drops into a busy bazaar. Voila! With the narrator's voice and visuals, we move from the world scene into the single bazaar.

This opening settles us into the mood, the time, the location, the culture, and the situation. We're plugged in and powered up for the plot.

That's what this chapter is about: powering up for what is to come. We met in the introduction—now, we're ready for our first marketing meeting.

When we power up and get the current flowing, we'll bring your business into the picture.

This chapter will put you in a marketing frame of mind. It will prepare you to introduce your business to others in benign ways that are unthreatening, disarming, and enlightening. Connecting and spotting marketing opportunities is often nonlinear. That's why getting your curiosity arroused is a powerful first tool. Then, we'll add the eight other tools. Feel free to come back here to recharge your batteries anytime. It's free.

Look Closer

We live in a multimedia world. The wireless revolution unplugged us from our desks and the phones from the wall. You may be reading this chapter in a bookstore, at a trade show, or in your car. Come with me.

Let's zoom our Web cam or camera lens into the conference room of a private high school, Tuesday afternoon, 2 p.m. Mary Lou Thiercof, my project partner, and I sit across the table from the president and the principal. Their recruitment video, their key marketing piece, needs an update. Their audience: eighth grade students. Our first objective: set the scene for them to plug into their audience's mindset and environment.

Students love video—movies, games, and more. They want action—the faster, the better.

Mary Lou and I smile as we turn to the president of the board of directors. "The new video will be peer to peer, student to student. We have an assignment for you before we start shooting," I say.

His eyes reply, "Where are you going with this?" Yet, we continue. We had to set up the tone we were proposing for the video, just like the camera at the beginning of the movie.

I take a deep breath and say, "Here's what you need to do in the next week: Watch five minutes of MTV."

The only sounds in the room are his eyes screaming. Two weeks go by. When we return with the completed video, he powers up the television. Click. It's on.

We watch with one eye on the television and one on him. No frowns. Good. No hands shaking. Better. No scratching his head.

Mission accomplished.

As he watches the final video with the quick cuts and short action sequences, he captures the perspective of those he wants to reach. He is now plugged into their worldview. He is, as movie character Austin Powers would say, "a bit of all right."

Zoom In

Words, images, and visuals stick. Well-written phrases punch, especially when they are sweet on the ears and candy to the eyes. Copywriters, screenwriters, and playwrights routinely plug into word and image power.

So will you with this first MarketSkill. It's time to explore and plug in to your environment a little deeper. You'll be surprised how enjoyable it is—and how valuable it can be to your marketing efforts.

A word, phrase, or visual from your exploring may:

- suggest an analogy to clarify a business concept.
- spring forth an image for your written or Web materials.
- spur an idea for an article.
- provide a conversation link to your services.
- loosen up your thinking.
- suggest an activity or an event.
- remind you to get in touch with someone.

Let's Get Busy

The following steps are set up to be as convenient as possible, to fit into your day easily.

Give yourself a week to do this.

Remember, when you plug in, you connect curiosity to purpose. You'll quickly gain confidence when you match marketing tools to marketing situations.

Ready?

1. The next time you're in the car, turn your car radio to a channel you never listen to.

If you usually listen to soft rock, try the hard variety. If the button to the all-news station is worn out, listen to what the sports fans are saying. If you love debate and talk radio, try some rhythm and blues. If oldies are your thing, rev up to hip hop. Just follow your ear.

There's an amazing array of venues to choose from: hip hop, alternative, classic or soft rock, jazz, country, rock, soul, oldies, talk radio, sports, National Public Radio, all news, multicultural. *Don't touch the dial for at least one minute!* Just listen.

2) **Turn on the television tonight at home or the one in your office this afternoon.**

Point that remote and click until you reach a station you usually don't watch. Here's a few possibilities: MTV, VH1, the Disney Channel. It you are really feeling adventurous, Nickelodeon. *Don't touch the remote for at least one minute!* Just look. You're plugging into a marketing frame of mind.

3) **For five minutes, peruse the headlines in a newspaper section you don't normally read.**

If you habitually read the business section, read the top story in the sports section. For example, as I write this, one of this morning's headlines from the *Los Angeles Times* reads, "These Splinters Were Far from Splendid." The story relates home run hitter Sammy Sosa using a cork-filled bat. Aside from the obvious ethical issue and the larger concern of betraying fans, it got me thinking. Splinters. Little pieces. Slivers.

That reminded me of a conversation with a prospective client last week. He said, "We need to do marketing in bite-sized pieces." *Slivers. Why not offer my services by the minute? MarketSkills by the minute.*

Wow. Reading this sports story created a great opportunity. Reading an unrelated area may for you, too. That's why I wanted to let you know about it.

If you normally read finance, be sure to flip through arts and entertainment. Read the funnies. You'll laugh, snicker, fume, smirk, or smile.

Read the ads. Let a catchy phrase catch you. Let a well-worded headline attract you. In the words of baseball great Yogi Berra, "You can observe a lot by watching." In this step, you'll find yourself observing more. That's the marketing current, the marketing frame of mind, turning on.

4) **The next time you're in a reception area and are trying to avoid bumping your knees into a table top full of magazines, pick up one you never read.**

Turn to the letter from the editor, the one that sets up the stories. Find out why the editor feels that the issues on page 117 are important enough for you to check out. The editor is plugging you into his or her perspective.

5) **Finally, logon to www.webcam.com and search.**

Search for a webcam close to home. I'm in California, so I like to look at the Golden Gate Bridge. See the cars speeding by; see the bikers on the walkway. Get plugged in.

If you're thinking, "Why?" read on.

Our goal is to plug into a marketing frame of mind and build flexibility into our viewpoints. You'll start noticing things and you will see more connections between your business and your environment.

"People don't always recognize opportunity," attorney Bob Field said to me over lunch one day. Bob said it better than I ever could. In the marketing and public relations field, we're trained to look around, to look for a "local angle" to a story, to link dissimilarities.

Do this first MarketSkill and join us. You'll take in the broad landscape and then zoom it, just like the movie camera. You'll break through the noise—your own. And that's a wrap for now.

Tool Tips

Concentrate—Let go of your to-do list for five minutes and zoom in on your environment.

Get *curious*—Let criticism sit on the sidelines while you soak in five minutes of new sights and sounds.

Make marketing *convenient*—Do one part of the MarketSkill today. Mark it "done" in the book.

Dare Yourself to Do It

Here's 11 more ways to plug into a marketing state of mind.

➡ **Drop in.** During lunchtime, drop into a toy store. (You can always be looking for something for a young friend.) Look at one or two displays and the offers. Notice what signs, sounds, or textures call your name. This will help you mix different senses into your marketing activities.

➡ **Brighten up.** Go to an art supply store and buy a large newsprint pad. Clear off your desk and cover it with individual sheets. Take crayons and draw a circle in the middle of the paper. Write down a key word to brainstorm about. For example, "visibility." Just let yourself go and write down any people, places, or things that come to mind. Use different colors. Hang the sheets on your wall and you'll see ideas emerge to heighten your visibility.

➡ **Tie it together.** Sit down with colored pens, a pad, and today's newspaper. You could be at the local coffee shop or your kitchen table. Write down key words from today's headlines. Now, jot down your key marketing message and see whether you can tie it to a headline topic.

➡ **Look out.** Watch MTV for 15 more minutes. You'll see marketing reaching out to the most fickle audience possible.

➡ **Flip.** If you have access to a flip chart, put it in your office with colored markers nearby. As you get ideas, write them down. Glancing at them keeps them alive. Or, if the flip chart clutters, put your ideas on index cards. Keep them close by. Flip through them once in a while. It may be the right time to implement one you've forgotten.

→ **Soak it up**. If you're working on your skills with a colleague, meet at alternating or different locales to soak in the energy of the environment.

→ **Eavesdrop.** Marketing is a very auditory discipline. I once read that singer/songwriter Smoky Robinson was in a grocery checkout line (I guess he goes to the store, too) when he heard someone say "I second that emotion." The phrase caught his ear—and his curiosity. Shortly after, he turned it into a top-selling tune.

→ **Steal a glance.** Look around your office and notice something new. Perhaps it's a book you forgot you had or maybe that toy airplane you keep on the credenza. Touch them. Sparking your senses sparks your marketing imagination.

→ **Forget it.** Eliminate one "should do" from your list today. That will free up some time and attention to play with these ideas.

→ **Say "Yes and."** The very first rule of professional improvisation is "Yes and." That means you don't negate what someone says; you acknowledge it and add to it. Put a Post-it by your phone that reads "Yes and ..." Try it in your very next conversation, especially when you're ready to disagree. With this tool, you'll sharpen your conversation skills, a must for marketing through personal contact.

→ **Scan want ads.** They present an across-the-board perspective on what people are dealing with. You'll smile. Guaranteed.

Marketing can be as rewarding as the technical work you do.
Have fun with these ideas to grow your business.

CHAPTER TWO

Raise the Stakes

David Clarke grabbed his coat as he glanced at the office clock. He realized he was getting home later and later.

As one of the youngest branch managers for one of the largest U.S. investment brokerage houses, he understood that "there is only so much production you can do on your own." He knew too well that individuals reach plateaus not just in income but also in personal and job satisfaction.

"I had to grow my business, but I had no more time," he says. "Time spent on the business was time away from my family, yet I needed the business to have the life I wanted my family to have."

This recognition, coupled with a business predator, the deafening onslaught of financial information in the market, identified a stake to raise. It was time for a new team in a new firm— his own.

No business lacks predators. Smart professionals turn them into opportunities and raise the stakes—put something at risk—to overcome them.

In this chapter, we'll talk with three professionals who raised the stakes and courted risks to satisfy their vision. Here, you'll discover how to identify and pick your most promising stake to raise in your marketing arena.

Raising the stakes is different from raising the bar. Raising the bar increases something without changing the underlying structure. You may do it inch by inch, client by client, in small doses.

Raising the stakes creates immediate motion. Jackhammer-like, it takes bold actions. You blast away at old paradigms, habits, and sheer inertia. You take decisive acts to shift infrastructure, you train to acquire new skills, and you may surround yourself with others who know more than you do.

Nature teaches us that nothing remains the same. Things either contract or expand. This principle alone provides motivation to raise the stakes and respond to challenges.

"For me," David says, "raising the stakes means change. Change is uncomfortable; I force myself to make changes, to put myself in different situations. I grow from it, and so does my business."

Commit and Create

No stranger to managing highly independent, creative individuals, David committed first to building the talent base he needed to compete professionally and complete his vision personally.

"Clients have major transactions that affect more than their portfolio," he says. "To reliably respond to these life events and financial needs, we must go beyond the numbers."

To go beyond the numbers, David's team sharpens its skills through weekly meetings, shared information, continuing education, and community outreach. The team members spend time together in workshops and revitalize approaches, test new ideas, and question old attitudes.

These activities raise the stakes for everyone with the goal: team integrity remains secure while clients remain content. A bold step, indeed, in an industry known to reward individual efforts and product-oriented approaches.

David is committed to the process though it isn't always comfortable. "You have to invest in resources before the benefit is there," he says.

Investing in resources takes commitment, and commitment creates opportunity. When the firm accepted 150 new clients from a retiring colleague, David reflects, "We couldn't have done this if we did not make the commitment to grow and put resources behind it first."

Watch for Shifting Scenes

Across town and across the country, business owners renew their energy and resources through chambers of commerce. You might think raising the stakes isn't necessary for an organization that has a substantial legacy of stimulating downtown areas and bringing community leaders together. But Jay Hoyer, a chamber decision maker for more than two decades and a member of the board of directors of the Western Association of Chamber of Commerce Executives, seeks out predators and raises the stakes as his primary choice to respond to them.

Jay compares raising the stakes to watching a motion picture. Images, sounds, and scenes shift in front of your eyes. "Can you see changes and respond to them?" he asks. "We had a focus group at a time when worker shortage was a distinct community concern. Yet, no chamber member said, 'It's your job to find us people.' Still, this unspoken need raised the stakes for us. We had to find ways to respond to the hiring issue."

To do this, the chamber partners with the city to promote the region, with local schools to enhance education, with business owners to improve employee benefits, and with government officials to make it easier to do business. As president of the local chamber, Jay doesn't stop there but draws on his national network to revitalize his outlook and garner insights from chambers in other parts of the country and Canada.

Like David, Jay seizes opportunity. "But it's not without risks," Jay says. "Risk is an unavoidable part of raising the stakes."

For example, his chamber offered a retirement plan sponsored by the National Chamber of Commerce. "Traditionally, we avoid offering any service that appears to compete with one of our members," he says. "In this case, none of our members could match this program. In fact, our board chairman encouraged us to move forward with the national option even though his own firm offered retirement plans." The board of directors debated the package, and they did offer it to the membership. Several chamber members quit over the loyalty versus service issue.

"Would you do it again?" I ask. "In a heartbeat," he says. "The value for members was there. Though it couldn't be met locally, it was our responsibility to offer the best option we could find."

Jay stresses that this was an acceptable risk, not a random one. "It's important to assess your risks," he says. "That way, if it doesn't work out, you can move on and still be intact. But you must take risks."

Sink Your Teeth In

Risks hang like a voter punch-card chad in the daily lives of elected officials. "The political world was a big departure from the business world for me," says former Assemblywoman Lynne Leach, who served three terms in the California state legislature. "Working in the political world is like herding cats."

Facing defeat in a first bid for her local council seat in the 1980s, Lynne could have headed back to her desk. Instead, she assessed the situation and decided to raise the stakes. She renewed her energies and built new allies. Lynne says, "I realized I had to become more sophisticated and have more contacts." This led her to Republican Central Committee involvement and subsequent chairmanship, a position she held for four years. In 1996, a state assembly seat opened up. She was asked to run. She was ready to raise the stakes even higher.

"When you run for election, you put your reputation on the line," she says. Once elected, the stakes almost raise themselves. "You represent your own issues, you represent constituent interests, and you quickly learn others don't play by the rules. We operate on 'your word is your bond,' yet it's common for someone to say one thing and do something very different. Some choose to take no risk at all and excuse themselves when it's time to vote." There is an abundance of noise in the political environment.

A former chamber of commerce president, Lynne, like Jay, turns sensitive eyes toward economic shifts. In the mid-'90s, she observed the predator of imbalanced economics erode students' chances to compete equally. As a freshman legislator, she introduced a bill to study fairness in education funding. It passed.

Now, armed with financial statistics, she made sure her next bill raised the stakes by increasing options for education funding. "Then, the trouble began," she says laughing. "The governor didn't feel there was a problem; narrow groups had their ideas. It didn't pass."

Lynne didn't stop there. She applied her junkyard dog philosophy: "Sink your teeth into it and don't let go." She held on and mustered support outside her district and across the aisle. She urged supporters to turn technology into their messengers to reach legislators. Bipartisan backing surfaced. The next year, California students received a percentage of the proposal funding increase. Throughout her term, Lynne continued to raise the stakes. Fairness in education funding went directly to California voters as a constitutional amendment.

Look Closer

It's clear that when you keep things constant, you contract. You lose touch and the ability to respond. Don't let that happen to you. Instead, like the trio of professionals we just met, look for opportunities to raise the stakes and hold on tight once you commit to action.

Does this mean you must expand your client base? Not necessarily. With minimal cost and time, why not revitalize your services, through technology? Why not add new services, through professional affiliations? Why not renew your services, through packaging?

Your underlying choices remain the same—expand, remain constant, or contract. By default, constancy becomes contraction, and contraction becomes demise.

Let's Get Busy

This MarketSkill triggers us to look at our environment, renew our goals, and raise the stakes. Set aside an hour to do this MarketSkill at a time of day when you are fresh and relaxed (maybe after a good workout).

1. **Identify a predator, a situation that could raid your long-term business prosperity.**

Here are some questions to help you along:

Is technology creating parity in your industry?

Are industries merging and turning your former colleagues and referral sources into competitors?

Does too much information lessen the perceived need for your services?

Select one "predator" to challenge.

2. **List five possibilities to tackle this predator and advance your goal.**

For example, could you:

- take on a partner, either through a strategic alliance or formal partnership?
- co-promote?
- obtain a new license or certification to heighten your positioning?

3. **Now, select one possibility that piques your curiosity, one you may have even considered, or one that you enjoy learning more about. This will ensure that when you "put it at stake," it will be high enough to thrill you and real enough to manage the risk.**

For example, David decides to expand his team of advisors. He is an experienced manager; this is an acceptable risk. Jay goes out into the community to learn current concerns and responds with new services. He is at ease asking questions and packaging ideas. Lynne introduces a bill to study an issue first. A solid win up front encourages bold endeavors down the line.

4. **Do two things this week to "raise the stakes" on your selected item. For example, if you decide to obtain a new license, buy your study materials and set aside time to crack them open.**

5. **Continue to take action until you've completely raised the stake. Once you no longer waiver in your commitment to the process, and you consistently take steps toward your goal, you have raised the stakes.**

Remember, no action equals contraction.

Tool Tips

Revitalize your marketing strategy with acceptable risks.

Renew your energy with new allies and viewpoints.

Respond to challenges with a junkyard dog grip.

Pointers from the Pros

Here are several successful habits to boost your commitment to raising the stakes.

Like predators, consolidation and liquidation slice the field of potential clients. In response, Marjorie Brody, Ernst & Young 2002 and 2001 "Entrepreneur of the Year" award finalist in the business consulting category and founder of Marjorie Brody Communications, listens as the corporate world reshapes its communication needs. "Video conferencing is on the rise," she says. "We have begun to invest in equipment and train our own staff to offer these services."

How does Marjorie keep her commitment renewed? Self-imposed deadlines are the norm. "Once it hits a goal list in this office, it gets done," she explains. "By the end of the year, we've hit 90% of our goals, and the other 10% gets done the next year."

For professionals who recognize that they need to raise the stakes, Marjorie advises: "If you don't raise the stakes, accept the fact you are going to contract. *Have the strength to know where you need help and hire someone now.*"

Jay Hoyer, the chamber of commerce executive whom we met earlier, attended a conference where the question of time spent in the office was discussed. He realized his in/out ratio was about 80/20. He decided to raise the stakes by reversing that. Now, he regularly and informally interviews chamber members and community leaders. *"There's no substitute for finding out what's on people's minds,"* he says.

Ask "What are you doing?" and "What's going on in your business?" and you find the next stake to raise.

Earlier in this chapter, investment advisor David Clarke talked about putting resources behind commitments. In fact, he keeps his personal reservoir of resources full. David is an avid reader of autobiographies and has spent time with leaders of industry (Lee Iacocca), government (John F. Kennedy), and business (Donald Trump).

He values imagination and communication and *urges other professionals to use them liberally.*

Former California Assemblywoman Lynne Leach underscores her philosophy on raising the stakes. *"If you believe in something, hang on like a junkyard dog,"* she says.

When professionals stall in their quest to revitalize their marketing activities, she suggests, "Talk to someone you can identify with who has already done it, even if you don't know them." If your venture doesn't work out, she says: "You'll learn something. Listening to new ideas may open doors for you."

Dare Yourself to Do It

One of the greatest word builders, William Shakespeare, in Sonnet 23, says, "...strength's abundance weakens his own heart." Abundance makes us comfortable. Comfort levels close our minds to risk, to reaching out, to consciously raising the stakes. Don't let that happen to you.

Take one of these ideas—just one—and act on it. Today.

➜ **Co-promote.** Launch a strategic alliance with this simple step. Put your business cards in the reception area of a colleague with an allied service and display his or hers in yours. If you work from home, co-market on your websites.

➜ **Swap seats.** Sign up for a volunteer committee you normally wouldn't sit on. For example, if you are a design person, offer to serve on the finance committee.

→ **Turn pages.** Read a magazine totally outside of your industry. Find a "best" practice in that industry that intrigues you. Find one way to adopt this practice in your business.

→ **Zoom in.** Let your strategic partners express their ideas about expansion and teamwork. Assess their merit in a separate discussion.

→ **Ask.** Set up time to talk with your colleagues about raising the stakes. Delve into how personal preferences affect viewpoints about change.

→ **Step up.** Offer to give a presentation to a civic group. The group interaction will enlighten you and suggest areas in which to take new action.

→ **Go retro.** Dig up your library card—and a tape player. Browse through your library's audiotape selection (you may be able to do it online). Listen to one tape outside your business area.

→ **Get physical.** Did you ever notice how habit causes things to disappear? We sit in the same chair, at the same desk, with the same view. After a while, we don't notice what's around us. Things become invisible.

Move your furniture and you'll move your mind, see things anew, and literally change your viewpoint. Another option: work in a different space. If you normally work at a desk, try a table.

→ **Timelock.** This is movie speak for setting a time limit. "We have only 30 seconds to detonate ..."— that's a timelock. Motivate yourself with a timelock for the above activities.

→ **Pick your own brain.** Go through your desk and find your idea file, the one with articles that intrigued you and graphics, stories, or inspirational pieces you might "use one day." Pick one idea that contributes to the stake you've selected to raise. Act on it.

→ **Sign up.** Sign up for a volunteer leadership position the next time you are asked. Don't worry about "being ready." You'll receive all the help you need from those asking, and you'll be amazed at just how ready you are.

CHAPTER THREE

Tee Off

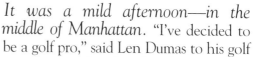

It was a mild afternoon—in the middle of Manhattan. "I've decided to be a golf pro," said Len Dumas to his golf coach as he placed his bag into the stand on the driving range.

"You can't do it," his coach said. "You would have to quit your job. You'll have no money and no time to practice."

The young golfer, who is now the head golf professional at a prominent San Francisco Bay Area country club today, smiled and nodded his head.

"You're right."

He then quit his full-time job as an accountant and moved to San Jose, California.

He sold his Mercedes, got a part-time accounting job and a full-time job at the local pro shop where he played, and he teed off to golf professional certification.

Halfway through this journey, he fell in love and moved to Minnesota for two years.

"How do people play golf in Minnesota?" I asked.

"Very quickly," he replied.

Len didn't become a golf professional by calendaring out his every move. First and foremost, he had to give himself time to excel at the game and learn the industry without self-incrimination or second-guessing. He had to focus; he had to break through the noise—his own.

"I was on a very tight budget, with little time for social activities," he says. Yet, he found freedoms within the new structure dictated by his decision. "I identified and overcame the obstacles."

How? Through interest—and marketing. To maintain his focus, he marketed to an audience of one: himself.

Model Winning Ways

Chances are you picked up this book to discover new ways to break old routines. You've made a commitment to power up or recharge your marketing skills. Bravo.

In this chapter, you will learn how to enjoy the marketing process and add personal power to continue it.

How? By doing what the pros do: practice, play, and prevent catastrophe.

As a PGA Class A golf instructor, Len observes: "In a game, people crave obstacles. But in the reality of the moment, for example, facing a water hazard, they retreat."

A water hazard is a significant obstacle for the unprepared. "You can't walk away from it," says Len. "Instead, develop options and skills to not only power through it but also flex your power of choice to handle it.

"Sharpen your game by working on your game—without pressure," he says. In other words, practice. Let's apply this to marketing.

No one wants to practice or at least admit that we do. We're already pros at our profession. So are world-class athletes who practice, train, and rehearse plays all the way to the top—in fact, that's the part we want to witness, isn't it? The warm-up on the ice minutes before the whistle, the spring-training camps, the inside look at weight-lifting workouts. On the plus side, as Len points out, practice relieves pressure.

Golf professional Jacque Vigil agrees. Jacque, who played on tour for almost a decade, observes, "When on tour, you see what people choose to do after a tournament, whether they socialize or stay on the course and work on their game.

"Most people head for the lounge," she says. "Yet, the more you work on your game, the more you trust what you do, the more you can enjoy it."

Here's what happens when you don't work on your game.

I was at a luncheon with 30 other professionals. The host asked us to introduce ourselves briefly, an outstanding opportunity to stand out. A writer stood up, looked up toward the ceiling for a moment, and then said: "Sam is my name, whoops, ah, let's see ... let me start again."

What a catastrophe. It was clear he had a solid, planned self-introduction, and it was very clear he didn't work on it enough to finesse and power through the pressure of 30 pairs of eyes and ears looking and listening. If he were on the golf course, you would have heard a splash as his ball arched into the water hazard. Don't let this happen to you.

Sneak away to Success

Where's the best place to work on your game? If you're a golfer, the driving range of course. You've got your bag in the car. You sneak away, and after a bucket or two of balls, you're back in the loop and are feeling great knowing you're ready for the next tee off. Ready to transfer this to your marketing skills? All right.

Let's Get Busy

This MarketSkill tees up time to fit marketing into your day—and practice it without pressure.

1) Put your gear in the car, that is:

- this book
- a recorder if you are an auditory learner
- a pocket-size notebook
- something to write with, maybe a few golf pencils

Great! Now, your gear is ready. You can work anytime, anyplace. In fact, if you truly are a golfer, put this gear inside one of the pockets in your golf bag. You might be able to get in a few minutes at the canteen after the driving range.

2) Plan to sneak away two times this week. You decide where and when.

A great place to sneak away without going away is in a car. Our cars are big investments; they're comfortable and quiet, so why not just spend a few extra minutes there on your way home or between appointments? Just put your gear under one of the seats.

3) **Mark this page, and then select a skill from one of the other chapters to work on. Come right back.**

4) **Got one? Great.**

Look over the skill and set a mini-goal to work on for this sneak away. Play with one mini-goal at a time as you would with a bucket of balls. It doesn't matter how small it is. It matters that you finish the step or substep you're on. This frees up your attention and keeps your game fresh to pick up cleanly at the next workout.

For example, if you're working on how to nail down talking points (key messages, see Chapter Six), just pick one point. That's it for that sneak away.

That's it for this tool. Just reread Step 1 and start! With this skill, you successfully created a space to work on your game, a space that's entirely your own.

Shhh!

Still finding it hard to sneak away? Need a nudge? Call a friend. Ask him or her to nudge you to sneak away. After your friend swears not to tell anyone you're "practicing," sandwich your session. Call him or her when you start and then when you're done.

Tool Tips

Practice—Hone your skill level and command of your marketing skills.

Prevent catastrophe—Finish what you start by setting targets and mini-goals.

Play—Look for opportunities to use your tools, both in one-to-one encounters or face-to-face meetings.

Pointers from the Pros—Golf Pros, That Is

How can you take these principles even further to tee off your marketing day for success? Here's a few more tips from the pros on how they turn practice into play.

Golf professional Len Dumas links purpose to play. "It's hard to accept obstacles when they are not on your own terms," he says. *"Make obstacles your own by practice without pressure."* Len tells of golfers who, faced with a ball hit into a group of trees, see a "small opening in the sky," and go for it. "The chances of making it are incredibly slim," says Len. He advises working on the hard stuff solo—and slow. "Working on a technique purposely makes an obstacle your own. Then, you can predict and choose in the heat of an event."

In marketing, make results predictable by honing your tools so you can use them in the heat of an event or presentation without flubs, stammers, or hesitations.

Golf professional Jacque Vigil offers: "It's important to make a challenge positive. Don't say, 'I'm going to shoot this score.'" Jackie tells of players who set unrealistic goals and then fall apart on the first tee. "Games get better little by little. *Narrow down your attention to where your game is now and play up from there.*"

Translation? Start marketing from where you are. Whether you're powering up for the first time or recharging your skills, you'll soon be nailing down messages and moving from venue to venue as a golfer moves from hole to hole.

Former touring golf professional Bill Mead is now a retirement plan advisor. "When I get a client, I don't lose them, yet a typical marketing cycle is long," he says. Bill doesn't respond to time management; he builds stamina for the cycle by setting mini-goals. "It's easy to get distracted in this business. Working on mini-goals is part of your game. *Mastering mini-goals makes barriers smaller and keeps your eyes on the objective.*"

For highly competitive situations, Bill takes his "go for the pin" attitude into the boardroom. "When you are leading by two strokes, you know you don't need to be aggressive. But when you are behind, you have to be ready to go for the pin," he says. By working on the mini-goals, he is ready to launch an aggressive "go for the pin" approach on short notice.

Club Professional Mark Heptig takes strokes off his game with the power of repetition. "When I see someone returning to their full swing after we took the swing apart in a lesson, I ask if he or she worked on what we did in the lesson, he says.

He is met by a frown. "No."

"Yet, *repetition in training is key to success* on the course," he adds. "It builds good habits. It frees up your focus. It lets you set the level of your game because your swing is dependable."

Shim LaGoy is a third-generation golfer. As president of the northern California section of the Professional Golf Association of America, he encourages members to stand for "honesty, integrity, and fair play." Shim appreciates play. He's seen too many rules spoil valuable activities.

"Too many rules take away the game," he reflects. "Golf courses used to be full of caddies.

"They found balls in the rough, carried your bag, kept score, and returned you safely to the club house. They practiced; they thrived by play." He notes that today there are so many regulations, "caddies have almost disappeared."

Don't let that happen to you. Shim suggests: *"As your own goodwill ambassador and marketer, keep your plan simple. Don't be so rigid in your rules that your ability to practice—and play— disappears like a ball in the rough."*

Work on your market skills as you do your golf swing? Of course. Pick another skill from this book as you would pick a club at the driving range. Take it apart. Reexamine the concepts. Play with your words and delivery. Go over it and do it again. You'll increase the success of your game naturally.

Dare Yourself to Do It

There's room for even more play—more options. Here are 11 more ways to make marketing a game:

➜ **Get the sun out of your eyes.** Talk with a loyal client you feel you "know everything about." Ask the client questions about the most familiar things. It may lead to new views on situations you take for granted.

➜ **Pick up the ball.** If you're coming back to this book after an absence, just pick a page and start from right where you are.

➜ **Reach instead of react.** Select a business function to attend, call a friend, and offer to pick him or her up. Your friend will be grateful. You may find he or she otherwise might not have gone.

➜ **Have fun with the fundamentals.** Rearrange the order in which you present concepts in your standard presentation. Tie them to one another in a different way.

➜ **Shape your swing.** Select three venues to try out one of the skills you've acquired so far. Sign up and go.

➜ **Change roles.** Describe your services to colleagues as though you were purchasing your services instead of providing them.

➜ **Eye the course, not the clock.** It may take time to craft your words. Throw that clock away. Be curious about your next step.

➜ **Eat.** Have lunch with a competitor. Brainstorm industry issues.

➜ **Bite off boredom.** Just like you work at shaping shots and changing direction, select an element of your presentation. See how many ways you can improve its impact.

➜ **Inventory ideas.** Talk with colleagues or clients in an industry that is most unlike yours. Find out one marketing idea that works for them; see how you can adapt it to your business.

➜ **Choose challenge over predictability.** Just as there are bunkers, water, elevation, and distance in a golf game, you've got numerous calls, contacts, and materials to work on in the game of business. Pick one and start!

CHAPTER FOUR

Get a Grip

What is control really about?

Have you ever considered whether you can control…

Who will call and say, "I'm ready to sign up for your service."?

What envelopes will arrive today with large orders or checks?

Who will inherit money and invest it with you if you are a financial advisor?

Who will wake up and decide this is the day to start a nutrition program and call you, their health coach or chiropractor?

Here's a few more. Can you control …

How many e-mails you'll originate today?

How many calls you'll make this week?

How many materials you'll send out this month?

How did you do? "No" to each of the first group? "Yes" to each of the second?

The first group of events you cannot control. The actual occurrence isn't under your total direction. The second group—yes—without a doubt, you control their content, timing, and pace.

This chapter is going to help you control an element critical to break through the noise and propel your marketing message: getting a grip on a prospective client's attention.

Whether you're raising the stakes in your business, just starting out, or transitioning from the corporate world to private practice, you've got to introduce yourself. We all yawn when we hear "I'm a…" or "I'm in …" unless it's a very dramatic profession such as a scuba diver, jockey, or animal trainer.

Yet, you can get the same response that these professionals do by combining what you do with who you are through a tool called a "talking tagline." As consumers, we've inherited hundreds of tag lines, those phrases that literally tag along with a logo. Add voice to an identifying phrase and you've got a talking tagline.

In conversation, a strong, colorful talking tagline invites interest and offers a fast understanding of your skills and talents. It generates interest right up front and translates your value into words that differentiate you from other professionals in your industry. It impacts your listener, whether an acquaintance or a potential client. Your listener grasps what is out of the ordinary that you bring to your clients.

The talking tagline also gets an immediate response—in a nontechnical, informative way, like your name.

From Technical to Tagline

Meet Bill Cruise, 5'11", easy-to-talk-to eyes, a radio voice. As president of an international engineering company, he resides in an industry that paces faster than champion racehorses on a dry track. "We connect computers in factories," he explains. "The precision and detail required by computer technology drives our future." After two-plus decades in business, at the time of our interview, he sees people subject to more clamor and clatter then ever. He says:

> "Our business environment is noisy. We meet prospective clients at trade shows and conventions. The unique part of our offer runs the risk of getting folded into the same program everyone else has. Cell phones ring, pagers go off, and people interrupt. We have to simplify our message. We have to find a way to say, 'Hey, we really are different.' When you say the words, they've got to grip. And you've got 500 milliseconds to say them in."

Does this sound familiar? Mix the blare of business with so-what attitudes, and people's attention is undeniably at a premium.

Bill's Solution

Bill believes he has found a solution. He says:

> "We set about examining what we do. A lot of information flows on the factory floor. What's the real value here? This information fuels decisions upstairs in the management suite. But it's not just about collecting information. It has to make sense, and it has to make money.
>
> "From a talking tagline prospective, we recognize we make data pay. *Make industrial data pay.* We started to use these simple words at functions. They gripped attention. Prospective clients wanted to know more. As a result, we began to get more referrals and better word of mouth."

Look Closer

Let's take a closer look at Bill's realization and his introduction. He went beyond the obvious "We connect computers in factories." He plugged into the power of purpose by answering the question "What purpose do we achieve?"

Notice that his description is simple and service oriented:

"We make industrial data pay."

With these few robust words, he describes a concept technical listeners easily grasp. The words arouse curiosity and connect to a potential client's purpose. The result is that the prospective client wants to know more—the hallmark of an effective talking tagline.

When a prospective client asks, "How do you do that?" the stage is set. Bill's talking tagline takes him directly to an expanded description or story.

"We connect computers in factories and extract information from them. Through this network, executives boost production and profits."

If you frequently use technical terms to describe your business, take a tip from Bill: "At first I hesitated to use a talking tagline. It was hard to do, very uncomfortable. However, once I heard, 'How do you do that?' I realized how simple and effective it is. I use it all the time now."

A Word about Verbs

Constance Hale, author of *Wired Style* and *Sin & Syntax*, writes, "Verbs add drama… They also kick-start sentences: without them, words simply cluster together in suspended animation, waiting for something to click."

Verbs invite story into your talking tagline.

Do you already have a talking tag? If so, why not refresh and reverse your perspective on it? Give it to someone else. Note your reaction when he or she says it and then use this MarketSkill to tighten up your grip on it.

If you are launching one now, ask someone to interview you by using the steps below. If no one is available, record your answers. Listen for action words and verbs.

Let's Get Busy

If we were sitting together, I'd ask you to tell me about your business. Within your answer, I'd find out what realm of activity your business falls into. It would increase, decrease, or maintain something. That's the secret of all good marketing and public relations campaigns. The first step is to define whether we want more of something (more people using cell phone headsets), less of something (less traffic), or maintain something (meeting with clients once a quarter).

Your business has a natural emphasis. Let's fit that into your talking tagline.

Write or record the answers to the following:

1. **Write down *what* your service increases, maintains, or decreases.**

   For example:

   > *increase* production
   > *maintain* energy
   > *lower* costs

2. **Turn to "Get a Grip with Power Verbs" at the end of this chapter. Find your category and select an action verb to fuel the engine of your words and, therefore, your work.**

    For example, rewording the verbs in step 1:

    boost production (increase)

    sustain energy (maintain)

    slash costs (decrease)

3. **In five words or less, identify your ideal client.**

4. **Now, link these phrases together into a sentence.**

    I _____**for**

    _____.

5) **Say it aloud until your lips adopt it.**

6) **Test your talking tagline on five people. Ask, "Do you get it?"**

You'll know you're breaking through the noise when your listener asks, "How do you do that?"

Bravo! Whether you are talking with a prospective client, colleague, or new acquaintance, use your talking tagline. You'll get a grip on his or her valuable attention.

Tool Tips

Simple—Keep your talking tagline simple to gain understanding.

Strong—Use lively verbs in your self-introduction to emphasize action.

Story telling—Provide a successful example to demonstrate results.

Pointers from the Pros

Here are some contributions from professionals who not only use their talking tagline—but also have fun with it.

Financial advisor Eric Flett: "I help busy, successful people create wealth."

Public Relations professional Mary Lou Thiercof: "I transform images and words into identities."

Advertising marketing executive Penny Melrose: "I generate leads and get results."

Real estate advisor Tom Givens: "I turn renters into homeowners."

Journalist Deborah Grossman: "I write about people and places that celebrate food and wine."

Dare Yourself to Do It:
Have Fun with Your Talking Tagline

No time like the present to dare yourself to start using your talking tagline. Here are 11 ways:

→ **Swirl it.** Put it on your computer as a screen saver.

→ **Welcome.** Feature it on your home page.

→ **Give up the ghost.** Try it out at a family reunion.

→ **Greet.** Introduce yourself with it at your next committee meeting or business function.

→ **Autograph.** Sign your e-mail with it.

→ **Speak up.** Say it when someone introduces you at a business reception.

→ **Compete.** Hold a contest with a few colleagues for the most creative talking tagline.

→ **Change roles.** Have someone else use it to introduce himself or herself to you.

→ **Transition.** Find three ways to turn it into a question and use it to transition during a client interview.

→ **Eavesdrop.** Record and listen to it in the car or while you're working out.

→ **Act up.** Imagine or say it in the style of your favorite performer just for fun.

Get a Grip with Power Verbs

This section links from Step 2 in your talking tagline design.

Select a power verb from one of these lists. Over time, increase the strength you choose!

The following verbs describe services that start or increase. For example, *trigger savings*.

generate	get	originate
make	start	set up
raise	use	develop
nurture	raise	shape
spread	master	facilitate
multiply	earn	launch
strengthen	save	aid
intensify	command	ramp up
promote	conquer	capitalize
profit	develop	grow
inspire	produce	advance
stimulate	cultivate	motivate
trigger	build	boost
double	establish	support
earn	create	assist
discover	prepare	improve
find	design	add

The following verbs describe services that continue or maintain.

For example: *preserve wealth*

use	foster	preserve
impact	iron out	protect
keep	stay	continue
sustain	move	retain
encourage	uphold	specialize

Verbs from this list decrease or stop:
for example: *Eliminate downtime*

relieve	trim	delegate
alleviate	cut	break down
prevent	shrink	eliminate
simplify	ease	divide
lessen	slash	avoid
diminish	minimize	stop
decrease	reduce	

CHAPTER FIVE

Gauge Receptivity

As you turn off your cell phone and tune in to your favorite radio station on the freeway, you hear, "In a recent interview with Robert De Niro…" Hmmm. That familiar voice fills your car. "I get to know my characters by"—BLIZZ—BUZZ—Huh? What happened? ZAP. The signal's gone. Just as the actor reveals his secrets.

Distracting, isn't it? No reception. Feel short-changed?

Radios and cell phones need strong signals, and strong signals ensure reception. Strong signals also reveal a potential client's or colleague's degree of receptivity. Without recognizing these signals, you may miss a marketing opportunity. Even worse, you may pursue one with little chance of success.

Gauging receptivity helps you level the playing field. When you discuss baseball, the economy, or an upcoming product launch with a perspective client, you both naturally search for clues. Is there an opportunity to pursue?

While you're wondering about this, buried beneath the social static is another question: Can you develop the craftsmanship to gauge receptivity and observe interests and needs of your potential clients?

Most definitely yes. Needs often parade as complaints or minor remarks. With "Gauge Receptivity," you will boost your ability to read signals and gauge needs through conversation, observation, and inquiry. You will fortify your efforts to initiate the next step with your client or prospective client, as insurance agent Tom Gavin did. Tom recalls:

"I just signed on a brand new client and didn't know her very well yet. I needed to get a signature on a document and planned to spend about five minutes with her to finish the paperwork.

"When I arrived, she invited me to sit down and then said, 'Tom, I'm thinking about moving out of the state.' She told me about her daughter who lived in Arizona and her son in Florida. She speculated about a new environment. Her eyes opened wide when she said, 'I think it's time to sell the house.'

"Through her comments, she revealed her need to increase rapport and share her views.

"My response? I poured attention on the quality of our communication as though pouring water into a pitcher.

"She wondered aloud if one of her children would get upset if she lived near the other.

"I looked at the paper I had come to get signed and asked, 'Would you like to hear how it works in my family, with my parent and sisters in different states?'

"We never discussed business. She called the next day and asked for a detailed proposal on a very large and completely different insurance need."

Look Closer

Tom achieved great success by not launching into his presentation prematurely. He watched his prospective client smile when she pictured a new environment. He saw her swallow hard when she wondered about upsetting her children. Then, Tom combined these observations with a focused question and story at the end of their meeting. The result? His ability to read signals and gauge receptivity created a strong foundation for the next contact.

Observe and Respond

Initial marketing contact is often made at business/social functions. It's almost 5:30 p.m., so let's walk into one. A chamber of commerce ambassador greets you and hands you a nametag. As you stick it onto your jacket (right side, so people can see your name when you shake hands), you walk past large potted plants and toward the conversation. The chamber's membership chair stands at the microphone and offers raffle tickets. You see Athena by the bar and head toward her. She faces the door as you greet her; she's looking over your head as you say "hello," obviously on the look-out for new arrivals.

What a waste. I better move on.

As you move toward the refreshments, you meet three types of noise: the unavoidable environment noise, the agenda in your head as you mentally tick off tasks, and the preoccupation of people like Athena.

Now, it's time to settle down and not fall prey to the preoccupation and distracting behavior you see around you. Though often accepted in crowded situations, preoccupation shuts off the fruits of observation.

Notice that while you are listening intently to your prospective client, a preoccupied competitor is looking over another's head for someone or something more "interesting." The same person in a meeting waits for the speaker to finish so he or she can begin. On the telephone, he or she takes other calls without warning.

To market effectively, assess your prospective client's interest. Give yourself a clear advantage over your competitors by mastering the tool of gauging receptivity. Remember to listen *here* and observe *now*.

Bob Field, the founding partner of Field, Richardson and Wilhemy, in Walnut Creek, California, says gauging receptivity is an important skill for attorneys. "This is something we can get better at," he says. "We often don't listen. We like to be listened to."

Looking and listening have their rewards. You begin to note signals, green flag go-aheads to begin marketing. You no longer have to ask yourself "Should I always attempt to market on the first contact—or never?" Such conflicting decisions dissolve in the face of gauging receptivity. Observing and gauging receptivity help you respond to signals—and fortify your efforts to take the next marketing step.

Let's Get Busy

It's time for a reality check. Ask an associate to partner with you on this MarketSkill. Assume you are at a business luncheon. Introduce yourself and begin talking about your industry.

Step One

Have your partner include three receptivity signals listed below in your conversation. When you observe the signal, check the box and continue talking until you observe three. Great.

Then, repeat the drill. Change and increase the signals as much as you need to until you feel you can confidently and correctly gauge the level of receptivity. When you are comfortable with this step, move to Step 2.

Levels of Receptivity:

1) **Asking *detailed* questions about what you do**
   Pass # 1 ☐ Pass #2 ☐

2) **Expressing a goal. For example, "It's time for us to gear up for..."**
   Pass # 1 ☐ Pass #2 ☐

3) **Asking for your business card**
   Pass # 1 ☐ Pass #2 ☐
   (*not* in exchange for his or her's)

4) **Becoming more animated when discussing your specialty**
   Pass # 1 ☐ Pass #2 ☐

5) **Expressing concern about a pending deadline for a service you can provide**
   Pass # 1 ☐ Pass #2 ☐

6) **Coming back to the subject after you have left it**
   Pass # 1 ☐ Pass #2 ☐

7) **Joking about working hard at something you could provide very easily**
   Pass # 1 ☐ Pass #2 ☐

8) **Launching into a story about an experience he or she had in your area that is still unresolved**
   Pass # 1 ☐ Pass #2 ☐

9) **Expressing an unmet need from the current provider**
   Pass # 1 ☐ Pass #2 ☐

10) **Relating an unfinished or incomplete project he or she "has been meaning to get around to."**
   Pass # 1 ☐ Pass #2 ☐

Step Two

1. **Think about the past few marketing events you attended and note when you missed an opportunity to gauge receptivity (Example: too busy with your own agenda).**

2. **Note one where you marketed too early and too aggressively based upon the levels of receptivity.**

3. **How would you handle these two situations if they occurred now?**

Tool Tips

Pick out the main idea of the person speaking to you. This sharpens your focus.

Perceive attitudes under the surface. They may indicate a good working fit.

Pay attention to needs. They often parade as complaints.

Pointers from the Pros

Newsletter publisher Jeff Rubin, of "Put It In Writing," recognizes receptivity when someone at a business function asks for on-the-spot advice. Jeff says: "After introductions, we'll often talk about newsletters, and the person will describe problems putting their newsletter together. Then, he'll ask, *'How do you do it?' With this question, he is opening the door for me to provide expertise."*

Jeff is not shy about providing expertise on his Web site. "Often, people worry about giving away information," he says. "When someone really needs your services, they quickly see how difficult it is to do it on their own. Referring them to your Web site makes them more receptive."

Francene Anderson, director with Mary Kay Cosmetics, markets at trade shows. Francene first creates receptivity with fun, informational questions about cosmetic use in general. When the prospective client offers a specific need, Francene offers a complimentary consultation. This perfectly illustrates two-way receptivity: create it and have an offer ready to act on it.

As a bonus, Francene rewards the prospective client for taking action. *"Every good prospect is a winner of something,"* she shares. "We always give a prize with a consultation."

Relationship banker MariAnn Leggat sees situational distraction and disinterest as good things. "It's easy to tell when someone just wants to get through the next few minutes at a reception," she says. "People walk by, and the person you are talking with looks at them while nodding their head at you. They're on autopilot."

Unless someone makes it clear that they don't have time to talk, MariAnn creates receptivity after the reception. She calls within a few days. "I saw you at the bank luncheon," she will say. *"There was a lot going on, so I just thought I would call to find out more about what you do."* At this point, she asks specific questions about the person's business and tunes her receptivity gauge to his or her attitude and answers.

Engineering executive Frank Napoleon recognizes that professional "technologists" are most comfortable in training environments, far from the trade show and factory sales floor. *Frank opens the door to receptivity with benign questions* such as "Are you getting something out of this seminar?" He ups the ante with "How does your company use this product?" Finally, he cracks open the eggshell of personal involvement with "What do you do at your company?"

Signs of receptivity along Frank's three-question highway include: *not* pulling their cell phone off their belt; *not* giving short, clippy, one-word answers such as "sometimes," "yeah," or "no"; and *not* searching for an exit with their eyes like a bird trapped in a church.

Helen Mendel, president of All Pro Promotions, served on the committee to bring the 2012 Olympics to the San Francisco Bay Area. At events, if Helen discovered the person she spoke with was not a sports fan, she offered a vision: "Could you see your child participating in a sport in 10 years?" She also created receptivity by wearing an Olympic lapel pin, guaranteed to light the torch of conversation.

When a prospective client gestures more and speaks more quickly, Helen sees her message is received. When she sees a sparkle in the prospective client's eyes, that's a plus—and a sign to follow up. Helen makes a special note on the prospective client's card and follows up in 48 hours with an e-mail.

Dare Yourself to Do It

In this age of rush and rudeness, barriers to gauging receptivity are easy to break—especially when your competitors are preoccupied. One of the best ways to gauge receptivity in others is to create it in yourself.

Whether you are entering a meeting or a reception or sending an e-mail, here are 11 ways to ensure you'll be ready to receive.

→ **Look.** Take in a room fully when you enter it by looking at the far corners.

→ **Respond.** Nod when someone meets your gaze as you walk through a gathering. It acknowledges this person and helps you "arrive."

→ **Include.** Take one step back when you are in a group to enable another to join the conversation.

→ **Greet.** Greet everyone around the table at a meeting, even if everyone does not greet you.

→ **Welcome.** Open every exchange with a "hello" or other acknowledgment rather than just joining in when someone opens with "I've been meaning to call you ..."

➜ **Encourage**. Ask a question when you find yourself losing focus in a conversation.

➜ **Get specific**. Mention a specific achievement of a community or business leader that inspired you. This opens receptivity channels on both sides.

➜ **Be food free**. Concentrate on communicating and connecting.

➜ **Shift perceptions**. If you are visually oriented, focus on sounds instead of sights and vice versa.

➜ **Open up**. At a sit-down event, leave one seat between you and your colleague. You'll both be more receptive to others.

➜ **Accept**. Recognize that others are gauging your receptivity. Relax and enjoy.

CHAPTER SIX

Nail It Down

You take your favorite CD out of its case, click "play," and listen. *I wish I could jam like that.* You lean into the music. *Wait a minute.* You listen a little closer. *I recognize that scale.*

A-ha! Don't you just love discovering the simplicity of something? Jazz musicians know that no matter who leads, they can't go wrong if they play in the same key. It's simple—but not evident when you sit with friends and tap to the beat at a cocktail table on a Friday night.

Want to unlock the code to wealth? Accountants know it. Everything you own less what you owe equals net worth. It's a clear-cut concept but not apparent when you turn to a 10-page financial statement with a folio of explanatory notes.

Want to be quick on your feet? Here's how. Say, "Yes, and…" —just like the pros. Improvisation actors never invalidate, argue, or change what their partners do. They power it with a simple "Yes, and…" That's how they get from cows to airplanes, from soap to satellites, and from the back seat of a Maserati to the shores of Tahiti.

Again, it's a simple approach. Great works of art, music, finance, and science spring from simplicities. Marketing springs from messages. Everything you do, say, write, and distribute springs from a few strong, simple messages.

To break through the noise, repeat your messages, accessorize them, add spice, and transform them into larger concepts, just as jazz musicians, financiers, and actors do.

This chapter, "Nail It Down," shows you how to use the secret of simplicities to drive your key messages and boost your results. It could be the turning point of your marketing efforts—so let's get started.

Turn Your Message into Simple Talking Points

Ray Peterson, the vice president of a major U.S. securities corporation, receives a memo informing him that a new investment program is about to replace the current one, his successful one. The new program radically changes the way clients pay fees.

He recalls: "Retaining clients was the issue. I didn't know how I was going to convert my current clients to the new program. There was no guarantee they would adopt it."

He spoke to other advisors in the office. Several had already begun to send out letters to their client base. He heard over and over: "We'll just have to take the hit." He knew if he just sent out a letter, he would certainly take a hit. At stake were thousands of dollars a year in income.

Ray knew his clients had to understand his message before they would accept the new program. But how? He turned to the power of marketing by simple messages called talking points to educate, inform, and help his clients decide whether the new program would work for them. First, research was in order.

Swapping Sides

He clicked on the television and watched CNBC from an investor's point of view. He saw the parade of financial analysts recommend "buy, hold, or sell." He surfed Web sites, picked up *Investors Daily*, and scanned several newsletters. *Now I get it. How could anyone have time to digest all this data?* He observed, "The deluge of information alone is undermining investors' ability to make time-sensitive, objective decisions—just the type necessary to fuel long-term portfolio success. It's noisy."

Hitting Pay Dirt

He identified the source of the noise. He got excited. *I think I can justify the change in this program.*

To communicate this discovery, he converted the top program features into three powerful, short messages—talking points.

The talking points resonated with his clients. "My clients manage businesses, travel frequently, and have important aspects of their lives to run," he says. "This program would help them keep their priorities intact. My research paid off."

After crafting the messages, Ray retained their simplicity and nailed them down through a variety of channels.

He related his talking points in four ways: first, by phone to his most important clients; next, in a letter; again in person when the clients came to the office; and finally, when they signed the papers to begin the new program. At the end of the program, he stated, "We had an 87% conversion rate."

Look Closer

When you provide a highly technical service, such as engineering, medical, or investment advice, you think in highly technical terms. You appreciate the technical distinctions of your service. Your clients and prospective clients often don't.

This is easy to forget when the urge to demonstrate your technical finesse lands on the tip of your tongue. Let research replace tech talk. Find talking points that nail down the values of your clients. It's easier than you think to convert nuances, technicalities, and laws of your discipline into simple, easy-to-receive talking points. Let's read on.

The good news is you can retain your technical integrity doing what you do every day—just shift viewpoints or swap sides. Read a medical newsletter with the eyes of a patient. Turn into a sponge the next time a client comes to you with "a problem you can handle in your sleep." Click onto that Web site clients keep mentioning.

Research. To a financial advisor, research is a walk through a framed-out portfolio; to a chiropractor, it is a look inside an exercise program started but dropped; to a consultant, it is a tour through incomplete expansion plans.

Research. That's how you gain a broader point of view to design messages that resonate with the values of your prospective and current clients. Then, you're ready to turn them into talking points.

Research and Repeat

Instead of a client base, you may be managing a reputation. Here's how a public relations professional saved the reputation of a public agency and the job of a client through research converted into talking points.

Roberta Wong Murray, APR (Accredited in Public Relations) and a member of the College of Fellows of the Public Relations Society of America, specializes in helping clients craft talking points.

Here's what she relates: "Early one Sunday morning, I opened the paper and saw a spread that criticized our client, a transportation district. Local businesses had fanned the flames of the discontent. The agency head interpreted this as a personal failure. In fact, he was ready to resign.

"We advised, 'Stop. Don't panic.' We examined the article and, then, through research, designed a response with specific facts that spoke to each part of the editorial. Presented with this, the agency head had to make his final decision: fight or flight. He chose to fight, signed the response, and sent it off. It ran the next day, and the situation moved to resolution."

Roberta suggests: "Whether you receive a challenge in print or in person, step back and tell yourself, 'Snap out of it.' Then, roll up your sleeves and plant your position with talking points— one by one."

Whether you're in crisis mode or planning to attend a fundraiser, pack your talking points.

Here's how. Design talking points with words that retain *your* style, *your* tone, and *your* imagery. That makes it real. It's easier than you think. Take it one step at a time and keep in mind the words of Tallulah Bankhead, who once said: "Nobody can be like me. Even I have a hard time sometimes."

Let's Get Busy

1. Select a stalled marketing project or a new one you're ready to launch.

We'll use Ray Peterson's new project as an example.

Ray's Project: Discover benefits of a mandated program change and convert clients to the new program.

Write down your project.

2. Write down the situation that necessitates your project.

Ray's situation: He faces a corporate requirement he cannot control that could cause him to lose clients.

For example, situations where talking points power your marketing message include:

- raising fees
- introducing a new service or a new associate
- relocating in a new community
- transitioning from one company to another.

What is your situation?

3. Answer the question: *Why should my clients or prospective clients care?*

Now, it's time to research. Keep in mind that those you want to reach, your current and prospective clients, are immersed in their own situations. In Ray's case, to reach clients who would benefit from the new program, he had to look at investing from their viewpoint. These individuals know they have to invest, yet they are busy, flooded with information, and must act immediately and unemotionally to stay ahead of the curve.

Here are a few questions to help you assume the viewpoint of your intended listeners, prospects, or clients:

What predators are closing in on my clients and prospective clients?

What new challenges does time or technology present them?

What information are they missing?

4) Now, list all the answers your research uncovers and next to each, list how your service solves that point.

Ray's research showed:

- investment information distributed through the media is easily misinterpreted
- avalanche of information hinders the decision-making process
- individuals are living longer, changing portfolio requirements

The new program gives him authority to research and then act on a client's behalf immediately. This eliminates transaction delays and gives clients more time to pursue personal goals.

What does your research show?

5. Voila! Now, edit and you have talking points.

Ray's final talking points:

The new program:

- helps clients focus on their priorities
- offers up-to-the-minute opportunities
- takes pressure off of clients to make decisions

Your messages are simple. They will fuel your entire campaign. They'll inform across all avenues: print, in-person, audio, video, CD, Web site.

If this is the only project you do from the entire book, I guarantee you will receive your book investment back, many times over. Well done!

 Pointers from the Pros

Ah, the magic of talking points soothes the ears like music notes. Here are some additional guidelines to propel your messages.

"People assume too much on the part of the reader when they design messages," says Douglas Perret Starr, Ph.D, professor of journalism at Texas A&M University.

"It's the most common pitfall," he says. "They get too wordy.

Distill your message and then express it in 35 words or less. You can weave in the details later."

Roberta Wong Murray, APR, offers the idea that "it's important to degeneralize your message. *To be effective, you must be as specific as possible.*"

J. Lindsey Wolf, APR and Manager of Environmental Communications, for the city of San Jose, California (one of the nation's recycling leaders), nails down recycling merits and methods—in headlines and in residents' minds. It's easy to pick out Lindsey in a room; the wattage in her eyes would make Thomas Edison proud. Her message about messages? "Observe."

"Observation tells you more than any formal means," she says. "For example, it is customary to hand out evaluations at a seminar or workshop. Don't stop there. Have an ally in the audience observe how people respond during the presentation. Are they listening? Taking notes? Fidgeting with their electronics? Have your ally stand in the hallway and listen. Are they talking about your five-point plan? Planning their next meal? Watch facial expressions.

"You don't have to have a large budget to do this. *Team up with another professional and trade. Observation leads the way in message design.*"

Tool Tips

Research to experience your message from the viewpoint of your audience.

Resonate your audience's values in your words and images.

Repeat your message in a variety of forms to nail it down.

Dare Yourself to Do It

Now, it is time to pour style and taste into your talking points. Take a few minutes and have fun with these challenges:

→ **Browse.** Go to a large bookstore and select a consumer magazine in your professional area. Look for a "quiz" and do it from the viewpoint of a novice.

→ **Translate.** Select the key word of a talking point and express it in different parts of speech. For example, the verb "work" transforms into the adjectives "working" or "workable," the noun "workout," and the phrase "the works."

→ **Check it out.** Select a Web site and look at it from the viewpoint of your target clients.

→ **Q & A.** Imagine you are a sole practitioner and it's time to add a new associate to your practice. Answer this: "Why should I (as a client) switch over to the new associate?" Boil this answer down to one talking point. Does it reflect the value of your current and prospective clients?

→ **Push record.** Pretend you are talking with a prospective client, and he or she says, "Tell me about your services." Record your reply. Listen for the most unusual point. Write it down.

→ **Talk in threes.** Work your simplified talking point (from above) into your approach three times in the next week.

→ **Simplify.** Write down a concept in your industry that is easily misunderstood. Now, complete this sentence to demystify it: *This concept reminds me of...*

→ **Excel.** Write down one alternative option to your service. How does your service surpass this option? Now, write a one-sentence talking point that dramatically demonstrates this. Use it!

→ **Chuckle.** Convert one of your factual talking points into a humorous talking point. Challenge yourself to use it three times in one day.

➜ **Meet and greet**. Review your new client welcome letter. Read it from the eyes of a new client. Redraft any talking points that don't reflect a fresh viewpoint and generate appreciation in the reader.

➜ **Move in**. Imagine you just moved into town and you're looking for a professional who provides your services. What is the first question you would ask the candidate? Consider how you, as the service provider, would normally answer. Now, what can you substitute to sharpen your talking points?

CHAPTER SEVEN

Stretch Out

"We'll have the calamari, the artichoke-wrapped shrimp, and the potstickers," Grace said to the waitress. Steve ordered another micro-brewed beer, and Marge opted for a merlot.

"What do you think?" asked Steve as he took a sip of the cold brew.

"I think it went very well," said Marge as she turned around, stood up, and faced the six tables of smiling faces.

"Let's give it up for the trade show committee," she said. Clapping deafened her thank-you speech. Six months of planning. Little sleep in the last week—it's done!

Does this sound familiar? If you've worked on a committee or intense project, you know the intensity it requires, the energy it demands, and the relief your feet feel when it's over.

It was worth it though, wasn't it? You've accomplished your mission and, as a plus, built tremendous camaraderie with the committee members.

What's Next?

Let's fast forward a few months. Have you kept in contact with all of them?

I've worked on many committees and must confess that I haven't kept in contact with many people. There's a quiet understanding that our hipbones separate at the end of a project, and the promise of "Yes, let's definitely keep in contact" finely fractures over time.

We all move on. Why? Because there is too much "noise" in

the environment, too much blare from new obligations, too much echo from "must do." We fire up our next project, with no free attention to keep up our connections.

How can we continue our own marketing efforts and include the people with whom we worked closely into the spaces we now occupy? Without sacrificing one more thing? Without adding one more expense? Without upsetting our current commitments?

Architects through the ages faced a similar challenge: construct a building without upsetting the current environment, fit amenities into a fixed space without disrupting the flow, connect the past to the future. Like a day subdivided into hours, Frank Lloyd Wright was the first to break through the concept of "the house as a box subdivided into smaller boxes," which Spencer Hart describes in the book *Frank Lloyd Wright.*

Wright stretched lifestyle with "well-lighted windows that opened the house to continuous views of the grounds" and "plantings and outdoor fixtures designed for a harmonious sense of unity between site and dwelling."

Just as Wright stretched living space, you can stretch your business relationships—with dialogue. In this chapter, you will discover how.

First, would you help with a little test? Say aloud, "Let's keep in touch." It sounds vague and we-all-know-it-will-never-happen, doesn't it?

Now, say aloud, "Stretch out." What happens to your arms? They're probably on the rise. If not, why don't you stand up right now and stretch? Or scratch your neck and stretch those elbows high?

Nice work! You take up more space, reach farther, and breathe deeper. Your actions are alive, directed, purposeful. In this chapter, you're going to stretch—stretch your marketing purpose and value—with dialogue.

"Not new," you say? Right. This chapter isn't about something "new." It's about being effective.

Show What You Know

Like Marge, whom we met at the beginning of the chapter, your marketing challenge is to communicate something relevant to people you may want to market your services to. Do you have time to read publications that your clients or prospective clients don't?

If you do, once you find an article of general interest, what about the reprint rights? There has to be an easier way, you say.

Yes, there is. Show what you know.

You'll stand tall on the principle Scott Center and Allen Cutlip explored in the book *Effective Public Relations*: "Marketing is talking to a passing parade." Clients, prospective clients, and contacts may literally pass you on the street or in cyberspace at an online conference. With this MarketSkill, you can offer something to stay connected after even a brief hallway "hello" or cyber meet and greet.

Here's how. Stretch one concept into a year full of communication. For example, my own work in marketing and public relations springs from a simple perspective: *Marketing is easy. You can do it, too.*

That's it. I look for opportunities to stretch this one concept in dialogue that matches the interests of my clients and prospective clients.

In the next few pages, we'll identify and then work together with your concept. Dress it up, dress it down, wax it, polish it, question it, all the while maintaining its integrity, as great architects do with the environment. The best part of this is you don't have to have an avalanche of ideas to be effective.

Why does this approach work? Your wellspring of interest drives effective and relevant discussion. Your interest packs your concept with passion. Your communication will be original. And real.

Like love. Songwriters stretch out a concept all the time. Love: they sing about it; write, argue, laugh, and cry about it; steal it; kill it; abandon it; covet it; condemn it; misname it. There's no scarcity of it! Why tire when you can create a new take on an old subject?

Look Closer

Let's look at this tool in action. Architect Joe Bologna, AIA, doesn't advertise. He doesn't put signs on building sites. He doesn't market to the general public. He markets to real estate developers.

Joe must stretch dialogue from property purchase to nailing up the "We're open" sign. He says, "In fact, we market to get involved ahead of the property purchase." This is a substantial commitment, as plans can launch two years ahead of property purchase. How does the process work?

Contact, Connect, and Continue

Joe first makes contact on a personal level. "When you market your work, it's important a prospective client hears directly from a principal of the firm," he says. He monitors what target developers like. When he completes a similar project, he sends a project summary and a photo of the finished building.

He connects on an educational level. "We suggest, inform, and propose ideas to help our prospects make long-term decisions." Joe makes it a point to ask questions and follow up with more information—quickly. He has no patience waiting for answers from firms marketing to him, so he is readily responsive to his own prospective clients. "We offer facts and figures to show we are experts." This educational connection pays off, as prospective clients begin to rely on Joe to answer questions.

He continues to stretch and show what he knows. "I look for ways to continually feed information," he says. "One very effective way is to invite prospective clients to the office to check out new drawing capabilities, new computer graphics, or better tools."

Let's Get Busy

If you've been marketing for a while, you've contacted many professionals and received many introductions. Now, let's master the ability to stretch dialogue beyond an initial introduction or project. This skill guarantees you'll never run out of ideas—original ideas.

Answer this question. What excites you about your profession? What core concept or idea do you love to work on, consult about, read about, and defend? It may be the one that seduced you early in your career. Today, you look for more of it.

Write down your core concept/idea.

Now, from the perspectives below, you'll inspect this idea and study it from different outlooks or angles.

As you move from one angle to the next over time, you'll build an inventory of ideas to stretch your dialogue and your marketing message. Ready?

Angle #1) Pretend you are telling someone about a time you helped a client with this idea, how the client was when he or she came in (before), and the results (after). Write down what you would say. Name this angle "Is It Possible?"

Angle #2) Tell us why you're hooked on this concept, list why it inspires you, why you can't get enough of it. Name this angle "In My Opinion."

Angle #3) Decide it's a bad idea and write down all the reasons it should be unplugged, outlawed, and out of circulation. This is your point-counterpoint piece to angle #2, the "You Be the Judge" angle.

Angle #4) Tell us what happens when this important concept is omitted, how clients miss opportunities, how liabilities bare themselves. Name this angle "What If?"

Keep going!

Angle #5) Imagine you are a client asking about this concept. Your situation in life has changed, and you need information. Write down three questions you would ask. Answer the questions. Name this angle "Did You Know?"

Angle #6) Write down how you would explain it to your mother, who knows nothing about what you do. Name this angle "Once upon a Time." You'll know when to use it.

Angle #7) Imagine you are answering a question for a very

interested client, one who loves to know more. Write down your response. Name this angle "You'll Love This."

Angle #8) Write down ways a very conservative client could adopt this concept. Name this angle "Have You Considered?"

Angle #9) Fire up a search engine and find a quotation about your concept, or make one up. For example, I say "Don't kill a marketing moment; execute it." Name this angle "In the Words Of."

Angle #10) Take a question from your "Did You Know?" angle and uncover emotion. Ask him or her questions about it. Name this angle "How Do You Feel About?"

Awesome! You're just about done.

When you have a minute, count up all the ideas you've generated, and you'll quickly see a substantial amount of dialogue ready to stretch out, just like the tape measure in the holder.

You can stretch your one idea into:

- talking points
- articles
- e-newsletter tips
- educational essays
- sound bites

Here's an example of an architect using this MarketSkill to stretch the architectural concept of "big use out of small spaces."

Is It Possible? to create space without sacrificing furnishings? Such an angle would address placement of pieces, colors, and textures.

In My Opinion You don't have to give up aesthetics to maximize space.

You Be the Judge (point-counterpoint) Can we make space without altering structure?

What If you can't see it any other way?

Did You Know how big a small space can be? This could contain tips to convert multiple activities into one room, such as entertaining and learning.

Once Upon a Time Sherry hated right angles (case study).

You'll Love This "Ten ways to surprise with space."

Have You Considered? mixing art with electronics to make a larger space?

In the Words Of Leonardo da Vinci: "Who would believe that so small a space could contain the images of the whole universe."

How Do You Feel About? replacing your desk with a convertible table?

Tool Tips

Contact—Meet with at least one colleague a week.

Connect—Use your common interests to connect.

Continue—Continue connecting, using your core concept and inventory of ideas from this MarketSkill.

Pointers from the Pros

When you stretch, you reach for something: your toes, the top shelf, the perfect project. The first step in stretching your dialogue is reaching your listeners.

How do listeners like to be reached? Here's what several architects from around the country offered. Perhaps you'll spot an idea to stretch your own dialogue.

Architect Laile Giansetto, AIA, prefers hard-copy communication to e-blasts. She deletes any e-mail from an unfamiliar sender. She values tangible things to fit into limited time. "I'm more likely to read something preprinted. It acts as a memory trigger."

She recommends, *"Make information tangible so you can find it, especially on top of a crowded desk."*

The next time you bite into a Noah's bagel, perhaps you'll think of architect David Avila, AIA. You see David's work when you walk into a Noah's. David responds to message repetition, a tool he uses to stretch dialogue in his own marketing. He launched the firm's spring campaign of "great design every season" with springs bouncing on the opening page of Avila Design, his architectural firm's Web site. He repeated this message by distributing Slinkys at a business mixer the firm sponsored. David recommends: "Get people involved in your message. *Compared to advertising, people remember when you extend their experience."*

E-mail dissolves distances, and New York-based architect Ann Rolland, AIA, inspects all unsolicited incoming mail. She responds or not based upon her appraisal. (Thanks, Ann, that's how we connected.) "I assess messages quickly, so making information graphically clear is important," she says. "Write a quick note and attach it to a brochure or project postcard. It's a 30-second thing, and it will reach your reader."

As chair of the Professional Practices Committee of the Architects Institute of America's New York chapter, Ann advises practitioners to stretch dialogue with simple actions. "Speak up," she says. *"Ask questions and make discussions educational."*

With more than 100 daily e-mails and upward of 50 phone calls, Bob Desautels, President of ATI Architects and Engineers responds to personal recommendations from his staff and peers. "If you're just starting to build a practice, take your ideas into the community to connect with your target market," he says. "Civic organizations are great incubators. You get exposed to potential clients, and you brainstorm with the best. Work on committees and you'll find simple actions stretch your dialogue.

"Personal contact is key," he says. "The bigger you get, the bigger you stretch."

CHAPTER EIGHT

Get Sticky

Penny Melrose had a problem. She hadn't expected to need legal help. As president of a high-tech advertising and marketing firm located in Santa Clara, California, the heart of Silicon Valley, she cultivated a roster of leading-edge clients. Over time, she collected accolades for her prowess to generate leads. She developed strong relationships with her clients.

One day, one of her clients "just couldn't pay the bill." After exhaustive efforts to collect on a friendly basis, she turned to an attorney whom her associate Catherine recommended. "I felt very comfortable talking with Alex," Penny says. "He was pleasant and gave me some general information about how he could help me."

Yet, she wasn't convinced. So, she asked another friend for a referral and called the second attorney. "Unlike Alex, Bob immediately asked me specific questions about my situation," she says. "He related a similar case he handled. In fact, he volunteered a technique that would work in my circumstances."

What did Bob do differently? First, his communication stuck to Penny's specific situation; he didn't generalize, as Alex did, about his practice. Next, he demonstrated credibility with his story of handling a similar situation.

Though Penny's situation resolved without legal intervention, Bob is the first attorney to come to mind when she hears, "Do you know a good attorney?" Why?

He broke through the noise with valued communication and

information. Shashi Tharoor, the United Nations Communications Director, once said: "Communications and information is not an end in itself. It exists to make your substantive work successful."

In other words, discussing your work—making it substantive—is not just spin. It's a tool to help your name stick and bring about "Top-of-Mind Awareness", or TOMA. That's what this chapter is all about.

Think of your business. If you are a mural artist, does your name vault to the top of company owners' minds who want to beautify their establishments? If you are a banker, does your name jump off your colleagues' lips when someone mentions a need for more business resources?

If not, why wait another day? Let's make sure you stick in people's minds—with TOMA.

Why Does TOMA Stick?

TOMA takes success off the passive shelf and puts it into the hands of your most valuable referral sources—your clients and colleagues.

The old adage of "My work speaks for me" no longer applies. Witness today's mergers and cross-industry activities. Accountants manage portfolios, banks sell mutual funds, and insurance agents offer products beyond traditional life insurance and annuities. The people you depended on to "automatically think of you" may be your competitors.

And then there's technology. Technology equalizes the playing field of technical emphasis. In the accounting field, programs now calculate your lowest mortgage, your alternative tax, and your "what if" financial questions. Unless you specialize in a very unusual area, technical emphasis no longer differentiates you from competitors. It no longer contributes to top-of-mind awareness.

Yet, top-of-mind awareness activates referrals in professional services. Why? When you switch providers, such as your dentist, doctor, attorney, accountant, insurance advisor, or internist, it is a high-risk, low-rush decision. You have invested in them. You have confided in them. You have respected their counsel.

At some point, you experience a change. Perhaps your

financial advisor retires, your veterinarian relocates, or you reevaluate your insurance needs after a major life event.

Like Penny, you naturally turn to family and friends for a referral. You wouldn't think of the Yellow Pages except as a last resort.

Like Bob, you provide value to ensure your name indeed sticks to the tip of referral tongues. The tool to use: stories.

Look Closer

Stories stick; facts fade. While facts do give information, stories communicate the essence of what you do.

Doctors of Chiropractic Laura and Bruce Presnick tell stories— every day in a variety of ways. Walk down the wall to treatment room 1A. When you reach for the doorknob, you notice something on the wall. It's a letter from parents who selected chiropractic instead of surgery for their son's back.

Sit in their reception room. Pick up the big binder that lies on the table. It's stuffed with stories—you may relate to the business person/recreational swimmer whose ankle suddenly seized up on the flip turn. She was delighted to receive drugless treatment.

Now, open their newsletter. Inside, you read about the couple who averted divorce when one spouse received treatment that alleviated marriage-threatening pain.

Each story, whether on the treatment-room wall, in the reception area, or in the newsletter, is personal, people oriented.

Dr. Bruce Presnick says: "Our old philosophy was to motivate people to come in. Then, we would educate about their condition. Now, we educate first and then motivate. An educated person makes his own decision and is more committed to care. Stories help us educate. People remember them and where they read them. That builds top-of-mind awareness. Our names stick."

Banking executive Rick Wise knows the power of a story to build top-of-mind awareness. He creates a TOMA atmosphere by making it possible for others to tell their stories in a casual, elegant environment.

It is lunchtime, Tuesday afternoon. Eight business people sip freshly brewed iced tea at a conference table covered with a white linen tablecloth. Decorative plates topped with fresh California cuisine sit in front of them. "Welcome to our get-together lunch," says Rick. "Let's begin with self-introductions."

By the end of the hour, this mix of prospective clients, current clients, and community leaders exchanges ideas and plans future contact. It is not unusual to hear "I feel like I just made seven new friends" or "I'm planning a trip. The next time I need a travel agent, I know who to call."

Rick reveals his strategy. "We look for ways to make clients feel special and to meet one another," he explains. "If we bring together a prospective client with a group of happy clients, they see how they might fit in with our bank."

Top-of-mind awareness is reinforced when guests drive or walk by the bank and remember their pleasurable experience.

Here's a close look at building TOMA in a social marketing situation.

You are at an open house for retailer Jared Massy who just opened a new electronics store. At the reception, Jared introduces you to architect Josh Jamison. Josh is on the rise. You see his signs on construction sites all over town. As an investment advisor, you're interested to know him better.

Here's a conversation you *don't* want to have:

"What do you do?" Josh says after initial small talk.

"I manage pension plans for companies."

"Do you know the financial planner Derek Whitney?"

Not wanting to say "no," you change the subject. End of marketing opportunity!

Now, let's replay this!

"What do you do?" Josh says after initial small talk.

"The best way to tell you is with an example. Let's say you are a business owner who helps companies slash inventory costs. You have a pension plan, but it's getting harder to attract top talent, and you're looking for innovative ways to do so.

"That's where we can help. We design a comprehensive pension plan for the employees and map out a portfolio that matches your lifestyle and saves you taxes."

Before he leaves the reception, Josh meets another advisor who tells him that he is a pension planner.

Whom will Josh remember?

 ### Let's Get Busy

Traditional TOMA is built with marketing materials such as newsletters, brochures, audiotapes, CDs and videos. With this MarketSkill, you will build verbal skills to tell your stories.

1) **Jot down the name of a client whose success with your services you are particularly proud of.**

2) **Describe the specific life event or situation that brought the client to you.**

When you talk with a prospective client, describe the situation in a "let's say" scenario.

"Let's say you are a business owner who helps companies slash inventory costs. You have a pension plan. It's getting harder to attract top talent, and you're looking for innovative ways to do so.

"That's where we can help. We explore your goals and propose a plan that keeps the team happy and saves you taxes."

3) **Have your prospective client visualize you in action.**

"We kick off the program with bagels on a Monday morning. We explain that this is the first of quarterly sessions. Everyone gets a chance to ask questions and leaves with a program guide."

4) **Help the prospective client anticipate the solution of his or her situation by involving him or her in the process:**

"You can imagine how relieved the employees are when they realize we will meet quarterly to keep them up to date."

For flexibility, select two other clients in other service areas and repeat steps 1-4.

Tool Tips

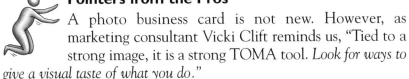

Create **Anecdotes**: Stories stick; facts fade.

Apply **Active** *verbs*: Let powerful words do the work for you.

Accentuate *benefits*: Let the prospective client envision the results.

Pointers from the Pros

A photo business card is not new. However, as marketing consultant Vicki Clift reminds us, "Tied to a strong image, it is a strong TOMA tool. *Look for ways to give a visual taste of what you do.*"

She cites the story of a client medical doctor who couples competence with openness. In lieu of a standard solo head shot on his card, the photo shows the doctor, dressed in a polo shirt with a stethoscope around his neck, smiling with a young patient. A fun moment. Competent. Approachable. Accessible.

Log on to www.fettke.com and you see speaker, success coach, and author of *Extreme Success* Rich Fettke in a business suit while climbing a cliff. That's Mickey's Cliff in Marin County, California, near popular Stinson Beach. Rich is also a record-holding extreme-sports athlete. He builds top-of-mind awareness with athletic prowess and storytelling finesse. "You can get stuck struggling in situations just like you can in a climb," he says. "Here's what happened when I couldn't get my footing." Rich applies sports-related solutions to everyday challenges.

He meets the challenge of heightening his presence in clients' and contacts' minds electronically. He stands on the scaffold of a complimentary e-mail newsletter. Each one relates a story, a dilemma, and a solution. *"Build TOMA with an offer,"* says Rich. At the end of each e-newsletter, you find a tip to examine your own situation and see how you can apply the insight to it.

With the trio of a strong Web site, strong stories, and a strong challenge in each e-mail newsletter, Rich never strays from his strategy of consistently building TOMA.

Director of The Power Etiquette Group and author of *Power Etiquette: What You Don't Know Can Kill Your Career* Dana May Casperson says, "A fast-track way to build 'top of mind awareness' is to say 'Thank you.'" She laments that fewer and fewer professionals offer words of appreciation; they are too quick to reach for their cell phones at the end of an exchange. Dana May points out, *"Magic words evoke response that affects attitude, body language, and emotion."* You can't wear them out.

Financial advisor Robert Shwedel drives TOMA continually. "Extend your stories to colleagues to let them know how you work," he says. *"If someone sends a client your way, do more than just call to say thank you. Take a bit of time to talk.* This simple action really sticks in people's minds—so few take the time."

Ursula Behiel, a top sales representative for a national payroll services company, employs tastebuds to build TOMA. "I will drop off the best cookies in town," she says of her regular visits to clients and prospective clients. One Halloween, her daughter dressed up in costume and handed Halloween candy bags directly to partners in client firms.

This simple, artful gesture tells a story of its own—*business doesn't have to be boring*—and it accentuates "Top-of-Mind-Awareness." You can do it, too. Read on!

Dare Yourself to Do It

Remember the first time you saw color on computer screens— how it caught your eye? The information jumped off the screen and generated interest. Let your TOMA tool do just that—in a no-cost or low-cost way.

→ **Archive**. Dedicate a place to collect TOMA—sticky story vocabulary. Add new words and verbs that strike you.

→ **Look out**. Watch five people in motion today. Write down verbs that describe them in action.

➜ **Cultivate**. Adopt a "Stories stick; facts fade" mind-set. Keep facts at your fingertips for later.

➜ **Invite to write**. Invite clients to share success by writing down one or two things they have realized from your work together. Provide decorative paper for them to write on. Put their comments into a binder for others to read.

➜ **Give it up**. Have "Compliments of ..." stickers made. Pair up with a colleague who provides an allied service. Put the stickers on informational booklets. Display them in one another's reception areas.

➜ **Ask**. Create opportunities for people to tell their stories: select one colleague a week and ask about his or her recent experiences.

➜ **Translate**. Turn a fact-filled piece of promotional material into one of the stories you created from the MarketSkill in this chapter. Include it in your next newsletter or e-mail alert.

➜ **Partner**. Team up with a colleague in a complimentary industry. Meet for coffee and help one another get sticky with the above skill.

➜ **Convert**. A thank-you is a testimonial in disguise. When you receive one in an e-mail, ask whether you can use it in your marketing binder.

➜ **Prepare**. The next time you receive a compliment, say "Thank you." Then, file it away for future story material.

➜ **Shortcut**. Direct several pointers to your Web site. If people remember your name faster than your business name, register your name.

For example, you can reach the Web site for this book through the author's name (www.elisasouthard.com) as well as the book name.

CHAPTER NINE

Recharge

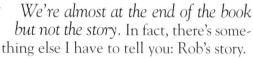

We're almost at the end of the book but not the story. In fact, there's something else I have to tell you: Rob's story.

Walk into the offices of R. J. Healy & Company and you receive a welcoming wave as Rob Healy finishes a phone call. A former athlete, he skied competitively prior to college. In lieu of a short-span sports career, he opted to climb the mountain to business success. Rob likes numbers. He likes people. He likes the stock market. In fact, he bought his first stock when he was 17.

In his 20s, he earned the Certified Public Accounting credential, CPA. In his 30s, he opened his own practice where he mastered the art of helping clients save taxes and simplify their businesses.

In his 40s, amidst an unrelenting media avalanche of advice, he began to see anxiety lines deepen in the brows of his clients. On their faces, he witnessed frowns. In their voices, he heard sighs as they struggled to explain what they had "just heard on CNBC."

When a married couple brought in their tax work, his observations became clear. "Clients have complex lives," he says. "They crave simplicity. They need more time to focus on business and families. Fewer advisors and more comprehensive advice would help."

He decided to make a change (one that may inspire and spur you to act in your own industry on your own behalf). He decided to recharge his interest in investing and specialize in investment management and financial planning.

As if on cue in a movie, barriers emerged. He challenged the traditional CPA role. "How would clients accept their accountant, who is branded with 'taxes' across the forehead, telling them what to invest in and, on top of that, suggesting they no longer need their broker to execute the buy and sell orders?" he wondered.

He thought of Mrs. Ferguson, a long-term client. He could already hear her saying "Why, I never thought of you outside of tax issues."

That's not all. He faced internal barriers: no one in the industry had done this and it was risky.

Instead of painting after work, he would head to the library. After months of intensive study, he would take several examinations for new credentials. How would these additional work hours affect the family? What about the time he couldn't spend on his boat? On his art?

While considering these questions, one certainty prevailed. Rob knew it was time to revamp his approach and redirect his clients' attention.

That's when he gave me a call. Let's see how he used the strategies in these chapters to transition a traditional accounting practice into a full-service investment advisory firm. We'll take out all the tools and examine them one-by-one. You'll be surprised how easily they propel one another, as a baton passed from one runner to the next.

Plug In

Let's see how Rob plugs into the investment industry.

In the car, he listens to investment ads with a new mind-set and plugs into offers. Reading the newspaper, he looks at investment articles with a new eye and plugs into approach. Meeting with clients, he opens with, "Tell me what you'll be doing when you stop working" instead of "Let's talk about your financial statement structure."

He gets curious. He asks broad questions and then zooms into specific client concerns and industry practices. He builds his marketing vocabulary and inventory of ideas. Rob is plugged in.

Is it time for you to plug into new approaches and practices?

Answer these questions:

Do you vary your information sources?
Yes ☐   No ☐

Do you let curiosity carry you away?
Yes ☐   No ☐

Do you use multi-media research?
Yes ☐   No ☐

"No" to any question? Recharge with the chapter, "Plug In," right now!

Raise the Stakes

What? Another software program, another advice magazine, a new do-it-yourself kit? Don't people know the value of professional services?

These internal questions led Rob to disarm a professional threat and discover a new practice-building opportunity.

As far as he was concerned, taking a risk was tantamount to building a new practice. Making the risk acceptable was the challenge. He minimized it with a combination of education and hands-on appeal. He asked, "What is it going to take to get the licenses I need?" He sat down with his wife and said: "This is the direction I'm heading. Can we work together on this?"

Like the professionals whose success we examined in "Raise the Stakes," along the way, he found new allies and new approaches to not only raise the stakes but also identify new ones.

Do you see predators approaching your business? Is it time to raise the stakes?

Answer these questions:

Do new practices or technologies prowl in your industry?
Yes ☐   No ☐

Is it hard for you to embrace risk?
Yes ☐   No ☐

Could you be more responsive?
Yes ☐   No ☐

"Yes" to any questions? Read "Raise the Stakes" right now!

Tee Off

The envelope read "Department of Consumer Affairs." Rob reached inside and pulled out the certificate that signaled "Good to go." After two years of study, research, and informal client surveys, he held his credentials in his hands and was ready to take action.

"I need a solid success with a few clients, and then I can launch a formal marketing campaign." Rob reviewed his situation. "I still had a full tax and accounting practice," he recalls. "I had to fit my investment work into an already full day, so here's what I found worked best.

"I set individual targets, like selecting one client who was ready for a change and who would give me a chance. I selected a client I knew I could accommodate without pressure."

He used the approach we talked about in "Tee Off." He selected one client to shape his swing, to practice without pressure.

That client was a software firm, owned by forward-looking Jennifer and Jake R. When they met for lunch, Rob offered this observation: "Jake, your needs are changing now that the business is booming and your employee base is growing. This takes sound investing. I would like to help you do that."

With that opening, he proposed: "I have spent the last two years gearing up to offer investment advisory services. I would like to offer them to you first."

The software executives agreed. Rob put together a portfolio and adjusted and monitored it as a golfer does a swing. "It was almost magical," he says. "As my interest in the investment area increased, I was less distracted and time wasn't a consideration."

How about you? Do current commitments barricade your dream?

Answer these questions:

Do you have a marketing project you just can't find time for?
Yes ☐ No ☐

Are you tired of traditional planning?
Yes ☐ No ☐

Are you ready to trade in a clock for an end result?
Yes ☐ No ☐

"Yes" to any question? Turn to "Tee Off," and recharge right now!

Get a Grip

"Excuse me; you caught me thinking about something else." Did you ever hear that? Here's what was really going on—you didn't get that person's attention. That person was wondering when to leave to avoid traffic. That person was thinking about when to take vacations. When you speak, break through this noise and generate interest!

The chapter "Get a Grip" tells you how. Here's a before and after look at Rob's new business introduction with the tool we discussed—a talking tagline to grip attention and launch conversation.

In-Person Introduction

Before: "I'm a CPA."

After: "I help individuals create and manage wealth."

Was his message perceived and received? You bet.

Next, we took his talking tagline to the front lines of contact—the telephone.

Voice Mail Greeting

Before: You've reached the accounting firm of R. J. Healy & Company...

After: You've reached the financial consulting firm of R. J. Healy & Company…

Signature

Finally, we took the talking tagline to paper and plaque— letterhead and signage.

Before: R. J. Healy, CPA

After: R. J. Healy, Investment Advisor, CPA.

These three steps reinforced his identity and message.

It's your turn. Are you happy with the response you get when you introduce yourself professionally?

Answer these questions:

Do you have a talking tagline—a unique professional introduction?
Yes ☐ No ☐

Is it easy to understand (simple)?
Yes ☐ No ☐

Does it emphasize actions (strong)?
Yes ☐ No ☐

Does it bond to a successful example (story)?
Yes ☐ No ☐

Is it current?
Yes ☐ No ☐

"No" to any question? Read "Get a Grip" right now!

 Gauge Receptivity

Here's the nightmare Rob didn't want to occur. A client comes in and has just come from the stockbroker's office and is eager to explain the broker's strategy while it's fresh in mind.

And he says: "Josh and Shauna, I have some big news. We're expanding services. We're ready to take over your portfolio."

Gasp!

This advisor knew better. Anticipating such a reaction from clients, he readied his presentation with the tool "gauge receptivity." First, he directed Josh's and Shauna's attention to priorities in their lives with:

"Let's talk about Morgan's and Madison's education."

Then, "What are your plans after they've gone through college and you sell the business?"

Through inquiries, he gathered information. Through responses, he gauged their receptivity. Throughout the discussion, he related his new credentials and his technical ramp up to the new service.

For hesitant clients and those who value routine, Rob assures them:

"If you are happy with the way things are, we'll continue just as before."

For those ready to go ahead, he launches into the formal investment interview.

These events took place *after* a letter introduced the new services and offered the same assurances.

If you've been wondering why clients refuse your offer or potential clients are hard to reach, step back. Is it time for you to reset your gauge?

Answer these questions:

1) Do you avoid business/social events?
Yes ☐   No ☐

2) Do you listen with a purpose during small talk?
Yes ☐   No ☐

3) Has a marketing opportunity slipped by you?
Yes ☐   No ☐

"Yes" to any question? Recharge with "Gauge Receptivity" right now!

Nail It Down

Armed with interest and receptivity, we're ready to nail down why Rob is the one to do the job. Let's convert his credibility into simple talking points—those messages that resonate with your client's viewpoint.

Clients are accustomed to dealing with three different professionals: accountant, stockbroker, and insurance agent. They need the assurance that their accountant, now investment advisor, has the same or greater command of investing techniques and specific understanding of their investment goals.

"One thing is clear," says Rob. "We can't fight the pictures clients have in their heads about the role we play in their financial lives. To them, we are tax advisors. We've got to close the credibility gap."

"Nail It Down" is the tool to use. As nails connect two materials, talking points connect concepts.

In this case, we nailed Rob's past experience to present capabilities. These nails turn into "talking points," key messages to secure professional trust. Here are the top five:

Rob's Story:
- *bought his first stock at age 17 and followed the market since college.*
- *performed his own research and still does today.*
- *earned a Bachelor of Arts in business with an emphasis on economics to guarantee a global market perspective.*
- *mastered financial statement analysis, the heart of any investment.*
- *cultivated opportunities from changing technologies and now helps clients do the same.*

There you have it, an inventory of strong, genuine, and active talking points to escort any client over the credibility gap.

There's even more we can do. Now that the gap is gone, we nail down these talking points in various parts of the prospective client interview. Here are a few examples:

"Ben and Carol, before we get started, it would be helpful for you to know more about my own investing experience …"

"Before we discuss your goals, let me tell you about my own investment history…"

"Here's something you might not be aware of …"

"You might be wondering about my own investment background …"

"Let me tell you how we've gotten to this point."

When you nail down your talking points, you educate, inform, and wake up interest.

If your conversations turn into technical explanations, ask: Is it time to recharge your talking points?

Answer these questions:

Do you look for opportunities to experience your service from your client's viewpoint?
Yes ☐   No ☐

Can you express the top benefits of your service in three simple messages?
Yes ☐   No ☐

Can you convert your messages into questions to draw out interest?
Yes ☐   No ☐

Can you repeat them in a variety of ways?
Yes ☐   No ☐

"No" to any question? Recharge with "Nail It Down" right now!

Stretch Out

 Let's assess. With the tools we examined so far, Rob successfully plugs into clients' realities, raises the stakes by offering a non-traditional service, tees off his program, grips the attention of prospects, gauges receptivity, and nails down talking points. What's next?

Stretch out. This chapter explores how relationships finely fracture as people move on and become distracted—by life, by the next project, by the next priority. It addresses how you can stretch your message to contact, connect, and continue interaction. You'll value this skill in times of transitions.

No one was spared a personal transition after September 11, 2001. Rob spoke with most clients within a week.

"At first, it was difficult to even think about calling clients," he says. "Yet, I knew I had to call. When the conversation turned to their financial futures, inevitably I heard that people hadn't had a chance to think about their investments."

When the client was up to it, he offered:

"I just wanted you to know we are holding our position. The work we did together, early on, when we set up your investment guidelines—those decisions will guide us now. We'll stick to those well-thought-out plans and keep our eyes on the long term."

Yet, he couldn't frame the message the same way for everyone. Using the tools in "Stretch Out," he matched up his communication goals with each client's requirement. Some wondered whether it was time to change. Some needed a gentle touch. Some wanted to know the full impact. Here's a small sample of how he contacted and set the conversation up to continue.

Purpose	Angle
Remind	*Have you thought about?*
Reassure	*In my opinion…*
Inform	*Did you know?*

These simple opening options gave him access to an important exchange of ideas. Dialogue stretches two ways. Both counselor and client reveal a little more of themselves and restore confidence in the relationship—and in the future.

Is it time to stretch out your message?

Answer these questions:

Do you have a core concept to hang your messages on?
Yes ☐ No ☐

Can you connect different viewpoints to your core concept?
Yes ☐ No ☐

Do you use a variety of channels to keep up dialogue?
Yes ☐ No ☐

"No" to any question? Recharge with "Stretch Out" right now!

Get Sticky

When clients leave your office, they fire up their engines. As they pull away, many tune into their favorite radio station. Between song or commentary, they hear advertising teasers. "Try us." "No obligation." "Guaranteed for life."

Your clients are active. Otherwise, they wouldn't be your clients. Don't take them for granted.

That's why your messages need to stick and counterbalance the avalanche of information your clients and prospective clients see, hear, witness, and hum all day. "Get Sticky" is your marketing maintenance tool. Let's look at how Rob uses it.

As the day's financial news unfolds, he makes notes. When he talks to clients, he's ready to discuss whether the market slips to a new low or rides to a new high—the direction doesn't matter. Questions and concerns do matter. He listens for questions, and offers an "In my opinion" or "Did you know?" perspective to illustrate how current events fit into the big picture.

In turn, each conversation reveals clients' outlooks. Each conversation expands his story vocabulary and library of issues to address in the future.

On a broader scale, he drives the industry agenda by bringing local practitioners together and by chairing statewide conferences. He is the "go to" person for peers considering offering investment services, and today, he keeps on top of issues as a member of the State Personal Financial Planning Committee for the California Society of CPAs. That's how he sticks close to the issues and stays active in the community. How about you?

If your messages and relationships slip away, let's explore. Is it time to "Get Sticky"?

Answer these questions:

Do you love the power of a good story?
Yes ☐   No ☐

Are you particularly proud of a client success?
Yes ☐   No ☐

Would you like more referrals?
Yes ☐   No ☐

"Yes" to any question? Recharge with "Get Sticky" right now!

You've Arrived

Ah, there you have it. You'll never forget the feeling of breaking through the noise when you put one of these tools to work.

They're now in your hands. Scan this chapter for interest, answer a few questions, and turn to the full chapter. Or take a moment to refresh a few concepts if this is the end of your reading.

This may be the end of the book. It isn't the end of the story. Please send me yours as you use and combine these tools to build your practice and promote your services. You can be sure I'm cheering you on. Break through the noise!

Let's Get Reacquainted

We meet again. Whether you've gotten here by sequentially reading the chapters or selectively sharpening your skills, you've made it. Congratulations.

You've experimented; you know what works for you, what rings true for you. All that's left is to take these tools wherever you go and use them whenever you wish.

Just one other thing I have to tell you. Business opportunities multiplied for me when I realized that business is all about helping one another. Commerce, though significant, needn't be serious.

Here's my wish to you as we close for now. Leave solemnity aside. When you power up, build messages, or recharge energy, have fun. Renowned playwright David Mamet reminds actors in his book, *True and False: Heresy and Common Sense for the Actor*, "You should go onstage as if to a hot date, not as if to give blood." What great advice to all of us. He counsels, "If it's not fun, it won't be done." I couldn't agree more. Let's not underestimate the value of simplicity, ease, and enjoyment.

At the beginning of this book, we overheard accounting professionals Dave Baker and Rich Moore resolve at New Year's to revitalize their marketing and public relations efforts. They did so with a tremendous amount of curiosity and sense of satisfaction. Dave was thinking about baseball when we tuned into their conversation. As this book goes to print, his son John is on the ball field playing for the Oakland Athletics' AA minor league team. Dave recently said, "He's building a career and having a ball."

May you have an exciting marketing life, too. Break through the noise!

References and Resources

Below you'll find beneficial references outside the direct area of marketing and public relations. Here are comments about a few of them.

Sin and Syntax is a joy to read. This book analyzes passages taken from literature as well as ad copy, and if you really enjoy the power of words, this is a great book to get you thinking.

Many theatre books talk about raising the stakes, but it was Julia Cameron's discussion of it in *The Right to Write* that sparked examination of that particular tool.

You may wonder why a book like playwright David Mamet's *True and False* is on this list. What he advises actors could easily apply to our work. In a no-nonsense style, this book underscores the importance of bringing a joyful attitude to your craft.

Art, by L. Ron Hubbard, has influenced me in countless ways, from stage presence as a public speaker to transforming simple concepts into fully integrated forms of communication.

Julia Cameron, *The Right to Write*, Penguin Putnam, 1998

Dana May Casperson, *Power Etiquette: What You Don't Know Can Kill Your Career*, Amacon, 1999

Scott M. Cutlip, Allen H. Center, Glen M. Broom, *Effective Public Relations*, Eighth Edition, Prentice Hall, Inc., 2000

Rich Fettke, *Extreme Success*, Simon & Schuster, 2002

Malcolm Gladwell, *The Tipping Point*, Little, Brown and Company, 2000

Seth Godin, *Permission Marketing*, Simon & Schuster, 1999

Constance Hale, *Sin and Syntax*, Broadway Books, 1999

Spencer Hart, *Frank Lloyd Wright*, Brompton Books, 1993

L. Ron Hubbard, *Art*, Bridge Publications, 1991

Dan Kennedy, *The Ultimate Sales Letter*, Adams Media Corporation, 1990

David Mamet, *True and False: Heresy and Common Sense for the Actor*, Random House, 1997

Regis McKenna, speech given to the Business Marketing Association, 2001

Peggy Noonan, *On Speaking Well*, HarperCollins, 1998

Don Peppers and Martha Rogers, PH.D., *Enterprise One to One*, Doubleday, 1997

Tom Peters, *The Circle of Innovation*, Alfred A. Knopf, 1997

Al Ries and Laura Ries, *The Fall of Advertising and the Rise of PR*, HarperCollins, 2002

Jack Trout, *The New Positioning*, Mc Graw-Hill, 1996

Roger von Oech, Ph. D., *A Whack on the Side of the Head*, Warner Books, 1983

Sergio Zyman, *The End of Marketing as We Know It*, HarperCollins, 1999

Other Resources

As your skills improve, your interests expand. Check out these organizations and Web sites.

Business Marketing Association: *www.bma.org*

Public Relations Society of America: *www.prsa.org.*

There are chapters throughout the country for these organizations, great people and important information to build on what you've learned here.

For business in your own backyard, get involved in your community.

www.chamberofcommerce.com provides local information about communities. You'll find this site helpful, especially helpful if you are relocating.

Join your chamber to gain leadership skills, build friendships and business. Your chamber participation and experience will prove to be invaluable.

To strengthen your public speaking skills, investigate *www.toastmasters.org*

If you speak on a regular basis, look into the National Speakers Association, *www.nsaspeaker.org*

Here are a more few sites to get your creative juices flowing.

www.reveries.com tracks marketing headlines throughout the country, and gives you a brief synopsis of the top marketing stories of the day.

www.picturequest.com has thousands of graphics, which you can peruse at no cost. Logon to the royalty-free section, type in a key word and you're off.

For research, *www.refdesk.com* helps you navigate other sites, and has a Google search link on its home page.

MKTG4U2

How often do you pick up a book and hear yourself say, "No, I haven't used it fully yet. I've been meaning to." If this rings true for you, why not work with Elisa and the MarketSkills team to speed up your results through:

- *Break Through the Noise™* workshops
- MarketSkills-by-the-Minute programs
- Personalized action plans

Your entire organization or professional association can put these ideas and tools to work. To get all the facts, call the MarketSkills toll-free number, 1-888-MTKG-4U2 (1-888-658-4482) or visit www.marketskills.com.

Think of the skills you have to look forward to!

Don't Forget to Download
Your Pocket Marketing Guide
... for FREE

Recharge and get more results with your *Break Through the Noise* Pocket Marketing Guide. It includes quick tips and handy reminders —a pocket tool to propel your success. It's included in the price and all you have to do is download it from the MarketSkills Website.

Logon to *www.marketskills.com*, then:

- click on Pocket Marketing Guide
- enter the user name: noisebreaker
- enter the password: propel

Thank you for choosing *Break Through the Noise* as your personal marketing and public relations tool of choice!

Meet the Author, Elisa Southard, APR

Elisa Southard helps professionals be their own best advocate.

Integrating marketing and public relations for over two decades, Elisa Southard's experience as a published writer, public relations/marketing consultant, television moderator, speaker, and community leader have made her a connoisseur of all the ways to attract new clients through personal contact. She is always ready to share tips and techniques.

As founder of MarketSkills, Elisa sparks individual practitioners and corporate executives to find the marketing talents hidden in their technical skills. As a speaker, she has presented tools and techniques to organizations such as the California Society of CPAs and The Executive Council.

As an author, her articles have appeared in newspapers and magazines including the *San Francisco Examiner* and the *Journal of Accountancy*.

As an arts enthusiast, Elisa serves the Diablo Regional Arts Association as a member of the Board of Trustees.

As a community leader, Elisa chaired the board of directors for two prominent San Francisco Bay Area organizations, the Walnut Creek YMCA and Walnut Creek Chamber of Commerce. She is the former Vice President of Professional Development for the Oakland East Bay Chapter of the Public Relations Society of America. She is a recipient of the prestigious YMCA Spirit Award.

Elisa graduated magna cum laude from California State University, Hayward, and is accredited by the Public Relations Society of America. She lives with her husband and pets in the San Francisco Bay area.

Index

strategic alliance, 14, 16

Stretch Out, xvii, xviii, 53-55, 58, 77-79

success, viii, xv, xvii, 15, 21-24, 31, 32, 35, 36, 44, 62, 65, 66, 68, 69, 71, 72, 74, 77, 80, 83, 89

T

talking points, 22, 44-48, 50, 51, 58, 76, 77

talking tagline, 28-32, 74

Tee Off, xvii, xviii, 19, 21, 23, 72, 73

television, xvii, 2, 4, 44, 91

Tharoor, Sashi, 62

The Circle of Innovation, 84

The End of Marketing as We Know It, 84

The Fall of Advertising and the Rise of PR, 84

The New Positioning, 84

The Right to Write , 83

The Tipping Point, 83

The Ultimate Sales Letter, 83

Thiercof, Mary Lou, viii, 2, 32

TOMA, 62-67

Tool Tips, 6, 15, 22, 31, 39. 49, 59, 66

tools, xiii, xvi, xvii, 2, 3, 22, 23, 56, 70, 77, 78, 80, 81, 87, 91

Top of Mind Awareness, 67

Trout, Jack, 84

True and False: Heresy and Common Sense for the Actor, 83

V

value(s), xvii, 12, 16, 28, 29, 45, 46, 49, 50, 54, 59, 61, 63, 71, 75, 78, 81

verb(s), 30, 31, 33, 34, 50, 65-67

Vigil, Jackie, 20, 23

von Oech, Ph. D., Roger, 84

W

Wired Style, 30

Wise, Rick, 63

Wolf, J. Lindsey, viii, 49

Wong-Murray, Roberta, 46, 49

Wright, Frank Lloyd, 54, 83

Y

Yes, and, 43

Z

Zyman, Sergio, 84